ECONOMIC ANALYSIS OF PROPERTY RIGHTS

POLITICAL ECONOMY OF INSTITUTIONS AND DECISIONS

Editors
James E. Alt, *Harvard University*
Douglass C. North, *Washington University of St. Louis*

Other books in the series
Alberto Alesina and Howard Rosenthal, *Partisan Politics, Divided Government and the Economy*
Lee J. Alston, Thráinn Eggertsson, and Douglass C. North, *Empirical Studies in Institutional Change*
James E. Alt and Kenneth Shepsle, eds., *Perspectives on Positive Political Economy*
Jeffrey S. Banks and Eric A. Hanushek, *Modern Political Economy: Old Topics, New Directions*
Robert Bates, *Beyond the Miracle of the Market: The Political Economy of Agrarian Development in Kenya*
Peter Cowhey and Mathew McCubbins, *Structure and Policy in Japan and the United States*
Gary W. Cox, *The Efficient Secret: The Cabinet and the Development of Political Parties in Victorian England*
Jean Ensminger, *Making a Market: The Institutional Transformation of an African Society*
Murray Horn, *The Political Economy of Public Administration: Institutional Choice in the Public Sector*
Jack Knight, *Institutions and Social Conflict*
Michael Laver and Kenneth Shepsle, *Cabinet Ministers and Parliamentary Government*
Michael Laver and Kenneth Shepsle, *Making and Breaking Governments*
Brian Levy and Pablo T. Spiller, *Regulations, Institutions, and Commitment*
Leif Lewin, *Ideology and Strategy: A Century of Swedish Politics* (English Edition)
Gary Libecap, *Contracting for Property Rights*
Mathew D. McCubbins and Terry Sullivan, eds., *Congress: Structure and Policy*
Gary J. Miller, *Managerial Dilemmas: The Political Economy of Hierarchy*
Douglass C. North, *Institutions, Institutional Change, and Economic Performance*
Elinor Ostrom, *Governing the Commons: The Evolution of Institutions for Collective Action*
J. Mark Ramseyer, *Odd Markets in Japanese History*
J. Mark Ramseyer and Frances Rosenbluth, *The Politics of Oligarchy: Institutional Choice in Imperial Japan*
Jean-Laurent Rosenthal, *The Fruits of Revolution: Property Rights, Litigation, and French Agriculture*
Charles Stewart III, *Budget Reform Politics: The Design of the Appropriations Process in the House of Representatives, 1865–1921*
George Tsebelis and Jeannette Money, *Bicameralism*
John Waterbury, *Exposed to Innumerable Delusions: Public Enterprise and State Power in Egypt, India, Mexico, and Turkey*
David L. Weimer, ed., *The Political Economy of Property Rights: Institutional Change and Credibility in the Reform of Centrally Planned Economies*

ECONOMIC ANALYSIS OF PROPERTY RIGHTS

SECOND EDITION

YORAM BARZEL

CAMBRIDGE
UNIVERSITY PRESS

PUBLISHED BY THE PRESS SYNDICATE OF THE UNIVERSITY OF CAMBRIDGE
The Pitt Building, Trumpington Street, Cambridge, United Kingdom

CAMBRIDGE UNIVERSITY PRESS
The Edinburgh Building, Cambridge CB2 2RU, UK   http: //www.cup.cam.ac.uk
40 West 20th Street, New York, NY 10011-4211, USA   http: //www.cup.org
10 Stamford Road, Oakleigh, Melbourne 3166, Australia

© Yoram Barzel 1997

First edition published 1989
Second edition published 1997
Reprinted 1999

Printed in the United States of America

Typeset in Sabon

A catalogue record for this book is available from the British Library

Library of Congress Cataloguing-in-Publication Data is available

ISBN 0-521-59275-5 hardback
ISBN 0-521-59713-7 paperback

1 0 0 1 7 5 6 2 6 9

Contents

Series editors' preface

The Cambridge Series on the Political Economy of Institutions and Decisions is built around attempts to answer two central questions: How do institutions evolve in response to individual incentives, strategies, and choices? How do institutions affect the performance of political and economic systems? The scope of the series is comparative and historical rather than international or specifically American, and the focus is positive rather than normative.

The first edition of this work has become the classic statement of the property rights paradigm. In this second edition Yoram Barzel clarifies, elaborates, and extends the argument. Clarifications consist of more straightforward writing and making effective use of diagrams to illustrate complex theoretical points. Elaboration takes the form of greater depth of analysis in various sections of the study; for example, the old chapter "The Old Firm and the New Organization" has been divided into two chapters that now include new sections on divided ownership and on insurance. Barzel extends the argument to the role of the state in the formation of rights, the role of government in lowering transaction costs, and property rights to wildlife.

The property rights model developed in this book is an important extension and modification of economic theory, explaining an array of phenomena that standard theory cannot successfully address.

Preface to the second edition

Since the publication of the first edition of this book I have continued to conduct research regarding economic organization and political economy. This work is reflected primarily in Chapters 5 and 6 of the current edition. I have also separated the discussion of divided ownership from that of the firm. The former now occupies Chapter 4, whereas in Chapter 5 I offer new thoughts on the latter. In Chapter 6 I briefly speculate on the emergence of property rights and the state.

Teaching property rights courses over the last few years has led me to discover in the first edition some errors, many ambiguities, and several instances that call for elaboration. I have attempted to correct the mistakes, clarify the exposition, and elaborate when necessary. I have also added a number of illustrations, some of which derive from new research on property rights.

I wish to thank Dean Lueck, who read the entire manuscript, for his helpful comments; my daughter Tamar, for enlivening the presentation and protecting the English language; and the Earhart Foundation for its generous financial support.

Preface to the first edition

The intellectual content of "property rights," a term that has enchanted and occasionally mesmerized economists, seems to lie within the jurisdiction of the legal profession. Consistent with their imperialist tendencies, however, economists have also attempted to appropriate it. Both disciplines can justify their claims, since the term is given different meanings on different occasions. Perhaps economists should initially have coined a term distinct from the one used for legal purposes, but by now the cost of doing so is too high. I attempt, however, to make clear the meaning I give to "property rights" and to demonstrate why property rights so defined are an appropriate subject for economic analysis.

The material of the book is at the heart of a course I have taught in recent years. Undergraduate students take my approach in stride. Graduate students often vigorously resist my dissatisfaction with the zero transaction costs model; converting them is, however, rewarding. This book is influenced by the diverse classroom reactions. It is an attempt to appeal both to those with little training in economics and to specialists.

I am grateful to my former students Douglas Allen and Dean Lueck and to my colleague Paul Heyne, who read early drafts of the book and forced me to reformulate many of my ideas and to clarify their presentation. Douglass North, who supported the project from its infancy, also read the entire manuscript and made numerous valuable suggestions. Victor Goldberg and Levis Kochin provided useful comments as well. I also thank Elizabeth Case and my daughter Tamar for excellent editing; they demonstrated that clear writing enhances clear thinking. Finally, I wish to thank the Earhart Foundation for financial support.

Introduction

In the slave societies of the American South and the West Indies, as well as in others, slaves consistently – albeit rarely – bought their contracts from their owners in order to redeem themselves from slavery. In these societies the law afforded owners virtually absolute rights over their slaves, only seldom granting any legal rights to the slaves themselves; consequently slaves were not legally entitled to own the property necessary for self-purchase. There was no legal barrier or authority to stand in the way of owners' retaining both slave *and* freedom money. Nevertheless self-purchase, whereby slaves acquired legal rights to their own labor, did occur.

As will be elaborated upon in Chapter 7, the study of property rights and of the costs of transacting can yield an explanation as to why slaves were able to buy their freedom; such explanations can be tested against the facts. The property rights model I develop in this book can provide explanations of an array of such phenomena, which standard economic theory cannot successfully address. These explanations range from identifying the reasons behind the choice between wage and piece-rate contracts to pinpointing the conditions under which charity is more efficient than profit-seeking behavior.

In the following chapter, I shall define "property rights" and introduce some of the central ideas of this book. In Chapter 2, the examination of the gasoline shortage of the 1970s illustrates the usefulness and importance of the property rights framework and familiarizes the reader with its mechanics. Chapters 3, 4, and 5 present the property rights model and its main organizational implications. Chapters 6 through 10 expand the model and apply it to various problems, including rights formation, slavery, and resource allocation in non-market settings. Chapter 11 summarizes the discussion presented in Chapters 1–10 and presents some general conclusions.

I

The property rights model

THE DEFINITION OF ECONOMIC AND LEGAL RIGHTS

What are property rights? The term "property rights" carries two distinct meanings in the economic literature. One, primarily developed by Alchian (1965, 1987) and Cheung (1969), is essentially the ability to enjoy a piece of property. The other, much more prevalent and much older, is essentially what the state assigns to a person.[1] I designate the first "economic (property) rights" and the second "legal (property) rights." Economic rights are the end (that is, what people ultimately seek), whereas legal rights are the means to achieve the end. In this book I am concerned primarily with economic rights. Legal rights play a primarily supporting role – a very prominent one, however, for they are easier to observe than economic rights.

I define the economic property rights an individual has over a commodity (or an asset) to be *the individual's ability, in expected terms, to consume the good (or the services of the asset)* directly or to consume it indirectly through exchange.[2] According to this definition, an individual has fewer rights over a commodity that is prone to theft or restrictions on its exchange.

The notion of rights is closely related to that of residual claimancy. The residual claimant to, say, an apartment house is its economic owner in that he is able to gain (here by exchange) from an increase in the value of the building, whereas he loses from a reduction in that value. Being its owner, he is motivated to take any action that will, net of its cost, increase the value of the property. The residual claimancy from an asset or an operation is often shared by several individuals. An important proposition, to be elaborated on in Chapter 3, is that in order to maximize the value of rights, a person's share in the residual should increase as his

---

[1] Ellickson (1991) makes the same distinction and elaborates on the role of the enforcement of rights without the assistance of the state.

[2] This definition follows that by Alchian (1965), Alchian (1987), Alchian and Allen (1977, pp. 114 and 198), Allen (1991) and Cheung (1970).

contribution to the mean output increases, and it should fall as his contribution decreases.

The economic rights people have over assets (including themselves and other people) are not constant; they are a function of their own direct efforts at protection, of other people's capture attempts, occasionally of formal and informal non-governmental protection, and of governmental protection effected primarily through the police and the courts.[3] *Legal rights are the rights recognized and enforced, in part, by the government.* These rights, as a rule, enhance economic rights, but the former are neither necessary nor sufficient for the existence of the latter. A major function of legal rights is to accommodate third-party adjudication and enforcement. In the absence of these safeguards, rights may still be valued, but assets and their exchange must then be self-enforced. Squatters are less secure in their rights to the land they occupy than are legal owners not because they lack deeds but because less police protection is expected for such holdings. Agreements based on goodwill are examples of exchange not supported by third-party enforcement.

As defined here, property rights are not absolute and can be changed by individuals' actions; such a definition, then, is useful in the analysis of resource allocation. The past failure of economists to exploit the property rights notion in the analysis of behavior probably stems from a tendency to consider rights as absolute.

The concept of property rights is closely related to that of transaction costs. I define transaction costs as the costs associated with the transfer, capture, and protection of rights.[4] If it is assumed that for any asset each of these costs is rising, and that both the full protection and the full transfer of rights are prohibitively costly, then it follows that rights are never complete, because people will never find it worthwhile to gain the entire potential of "their" assets. In order that the rights to an asset be complete or perfectly delineated, both its owner and other individuals potentially interested in the asset must possess full knowledge of all its valued attributes. With full knowledge, the transfer of rights to an asset can be readily effected. Conversely, when rights are perfectly delineated, product information must be costless to obtain and the (relevant) costs of transacting must then be zero.

When transaction costs are positive, rights to assets will not be perfectly delineated. The reason is that, relative to their value, some of the

---

[3] The distinction sometimes made between property rights and human rights is spurious. Human rights are simply part of a person's property rights. Human rights may be difficult to protect or to exchange, but so are rights to many other assets. See Alchian and Allen 1977, p. 114.

[4] See Barzel 1982 and Allen 1991. What Jensen and Meckling (1976) define as agency cost is what is defined here as transaction cost.

attributes of the assets are costly to measure. Therefore the attributes of such assets are not fully known to prospective owners and are often not known to the current owner either. The transfer of assets entails costs resulting from both parties' attempts to determine what the valued attributes of these assets are and from the attempt by each to capture those attributes that, because of the prohibitive costs, remain poorly delineated.[5] Exchanges that otherwise would be attractive may be forsaken because of such exchange costs.

An illustration of the costliness of exchanging rights and their effect on resource allocation may be drawn from the draft of college football players by the National Football League (NFL). By drafting a player, a team acquires the exclusive negotiation rights for his services, inclusive of the right to transfer to any other NFL team. Every year the twenty-eight NFL teams select eligible college players in a predetermined sequence. It would seem that the team with the right to, say, the twentieth selection would choose the player among those not yet drafted whose net value to *any* of the teams is highest. Given the diversity of both players and teams, the probability that the team with the right to the twentieth selection will also be the one placing its highest value on any of the remaining players is the same as any other team's, that is, one in twenty-eight. Were the costs of exchange among teams low, the probability of that player being traded would then be twenty-seven in twenty-eight. The observed trading frequency of newly drafted players, however, is much lower than a low transaction cost model predicts. This cost of transacting, at least, does seem to be considerable.

What underlies this costliness of transacting? What are the factors that prevent people from realizing the full value of their assets? Commodities have many attributes whose levels vary from one specimen to another. Measuring these levels is too costly to be comprehensive or entirely accurate. How difficult it is to obtain full information in the face of variability fundamentally determines how difficult it is to delineate rights. Because it is costly to measure commodities fully, the potential of wealth capture is present in every exchange. The opportunity for wealth capture is equivalent to finding property in the public domain. A commodity lies in the "public domain" when the resources needed to acquire it accrue to no one.[6] As viewed here, some wealth spills over into the public domain in every exchange, and individuals spend resources to capture it. This is characterized as "capture" because here, in contrast to a market sale, the original owner does not receive what the recipient expends. Whereas people always expect to gain from exchange, they also always spend re-

---

[5] Similar considerations (not elaborated on here) apply to the protection of assets.

[6] As discussed in Chapter 2, the waiting time that people spend in line to acquire a "free" good accrues to no one, and therefore such a good lies in the public domain.

sources on capture. Individuals maximize their (expected) net gains, the gains from exchange as conventionally perceived net of the cost of effecting exchange.

The sale of cherries illustrates the phenomenon of wealth capture. Obvious problems of information present themselves when cherries are exchanged. Customers must spend resources in order to determine whether a store's cherries are worth buying and which particular cherries to buy. Store owners who allow customers to pick and choose cannot easily prevent them from eating cherries after they have already decided whether or not to buy them, nor can they prevent customers' careless handling of cherries. Indeed, the process of picking and choosing itself allows wealth capture in the form of excess choosing.[7] The fact that the same cherry may be inspected by multiple customers indicates that some of the cherries' attributes are placed in the public domain. The high cost of information results in transaction costs – costs that would not arise were the owner and the consumer of cherries the same person. If information about the cherries were costless, their initial owner would not have to relinquish any rights, and pilfering, damage, and excess choosing would be avoided. In reality, such public domain problems are unavoidable; people can take steps, however, to reduce the associated losses. One of the main tasks I will undertake is to discover some methods to reduce such losses.

DIVIDED OWNERSHIP OF COMMODITIES

Net gains from exchange can often be increased if the original owners of commodities transfer only subsets of the commodities' attributes while retaining the rest. Cases where only a subset of rights is transferred are common; for instance, this is so in all rental agreements, as it is in any sale subject to guarantee. Exchanges that take this form result in divided property rights for single commodities: two or more individuals may own distinct attributes of the same commodity. As will be elaborated in Chapters 4 and 8, restrictions on the behavior of the owners may be imposed in order to enhance the separation of their individual economic rights. Incomplete separation makes attributes common property, relinquishing them to the public domain; if they are in the public domain, resources are spent on their capture.

Not only is ownership of commodities often divided; ownership of what appear to be the assets of an organization may be divided as well.[8]

---

[7] Barzel 1982.

[8] Alchian (1965) recognizes that ownership of commodities and of organizations may be divided. Posner (1992) discussed property rights; he, too, notes that ownership can be divided.

Physical operations within, and on the fringe of, an organization such as a firm usually involve many commodities and, correspondingly, many attributes. Several individuals share in ownership of the attributes, each owning alone or with others some subset of these. Stockholders own some of these attributes, but definitely not all of them. For example, a firm (or, more accurately, its stockholders) that has a service contract for a copier to which it has the title does not have full economic rights over the copier. The firm is not the only party that gains when the copier performs well and loses when it does not. The service supplier is the residual claimant from the servicing operation, gaining if it provides good service and losing if the service is poor; it is thus a part owner of the copier. Among other partial owners is the manufacturer, which is liable for certain damages the copier may cause. Others are the employees, who are able to put the copier to personal use without charge; they are also part owners of economic rights, though not of legal rights, since in practice they have a claim on some of the copier's output. Here, too, restrictions may serve to separate rights and prevent free rides. In Chapter 8 it will be shown that such restrictions do not necessarily attenuate rights but instead may enhance them.

FACTORS THAT AFFECT
THE ALLOCATION OF OWNERSHIP

One of the most celebrated propositions in economics is the Coase Theorem: When rights are well defined and the cost of transacting is zero, resource allocation is efficient and independent of the pattern of ownership (Coase 1960). Were rights well defined everywhere, much of economics, including this book, would be superfluous. Because the cost of transacting is positive, delineating and enforcing rights is costly – prohibitively so if done to perfection. In this section the proposition will be extended to consider the effect of positive transaction cost.

The ability to receive the income flow generated by an asset constitutes part of the property rights over it. The value of an asset is lowered when non-owners are inclined and able to affect its income flow without bearing the full costs of their actions. The maximization of the net value of an asset, then, involves the ownership or ownership pattern that can most effectively constrain uncompensated exploitation. The kind of ownership pattern to emerge depends on the variability in value of such assets.

It is relatively easy to ensure the rights to an asset when the service flow it generates can be readily ascertained, because it is easy to impose a charge commensurate with the level of service exchanged. When the service flow is *known* and *constant,* it is easiest to ensure that rights over the asset are also certain. If the flow is *variable* but fully *predictable* (for instance, if the service is the amount of electricity solar panels produce as the length of the day changes), rights are still easy to ensure, as they are if the flow is not certain but is *unalterable* (for instance, the amount of electricity the panels produce as weather conditions change). It is evident that, given the mean outcome, variability and uncertainty may reduce the value of the asset but need not affect the certainty of ownership.

When the flow of income from an asset may be affected by the exchange parties, ensuring ownership over it becomes problematic. When the income stream is variable and not fully predictable, it is costly to determine whether the flow is what it should have been in any particular case. Consequently, it is also costly to determine whether part of the income stream has been captured by the exchange parties. The exchange parties will engage in wealth-consuming capture activities because they expect to gain from them. When the income stream from the exchanged property is subject to random fluctuations, and when both parties can gain by affecting that income stream, the delineation of ownership then becomes imperfect.

A special case of great importance for understanding the circumstances under which ownership can be ensured arises when only one of two exchange parties can affect the income flow. Making the person who can affect the flow bear full responsibility for his or her actions ensures that ownership becomes secure. Such a person, being the "residual claimant" to an outcome that only he or she can influence, is the full-fledged owner of the asset.

In reality, randomness is pervasive and both exchange parties can affect the service flow generated by exchanged assets; ownership is therefore seldom if ever fully secure. For instance, the income stream generated by a rented car depends, in part, on how smoothly the car operates. Since used and even new cars are not identical to one another, they are not expected to run equally smoothly. A smooth ride is an attribute that both the owner and the renter can affect. A renter will find it expensive to determine to what extent the smoothness of the ride of the rental car results from its character and to what extent it results from the care given to servicing it. It is expensive to determine the true mean of the population from which the car is obtained, and it is difficult to know to whom to attribute the actual performance. Similarly, the owner cannot tell how much the smoothness of the rented car's ride has deteriorated because of the way it has been driven and how much it has deteriorated because of its character. As a result, the owner may skimp on servicing rental cars – doing less than owner-drivers would – and renters may be less careful with rented cars then they would be with their own. Each party expects such behavior of the other. Therefore, the demand function for rented cars will adjust for the effects of inadequate servicing, and the supply function will adjust for the effects of careless driving. The net gain in using the rental market, then, is less than it would be were the two parties to exercise greater care. If smoothness were costlessly measurable, the effect that each transactor had on that attribute could be easily determined and accurately charged for. In reality, assessing such marginal charges accurately is prohibitively expensive, and (maximizing) owners will choose not to exercise their rights fully. Some of the income stream, then, is left in the public domain. It is partly recaptured by the exchanging parties, who act differently than owner-drivers would.

Whereas rights cannot be fully defined economically when both exchange parties are able to affect the outcome, only one pattern of ownership does maximize the net income from the asset (and thus its value to its original owner). As I have already stated, the general principle underlying the maximizing allocation of ownership is that the greater a party's inclination to affect the mean income an asset can generate, the greater is the share of the residual (that is, ownership share) that party should assume.

The nominal owner of an asset may seem to have the right to the income the asset can generate. When the highest income the asset can generate requires exchange, some of the income potential will be used up in the process of effecting the exchange. The net income an asset will generate *depends* on the delineation of rights, that is, on how secure rights are over it. In the case described earlier, where only one person can affect the income from an asset, it is only when that person becomes the owner of the asset that rights become perfectly well defined, and it is only then that the income is maximized. This is a case where (as will be discussed in Chapter 4) rights are allocated clearly and income is maximized only under a particular allocation of rights. Since transacting is costly, the Coase Theorem cannot be invoked; it becomes meaningless to state here that as rights are well defined, income is maximized regardless of who has these rights.

THE RELATIONSHIP BETWEEN INDIVIDUALS' RIGHTS AND ECONOMIC ORGANIZATIONS

Alienating assets and obtaining income from them require exchange, the mutual ceding of rights. Contracts that delineate the terms under which legal rights are exchanged govern much of the exchange of economic property rights and are central to the study of such rights. Some contracting parties consist of individuals acting on their own behalf. Others consist of pairs of organizations such as firms, governments, clubs, and families. In addition, there are contracts between individuals and such organizations. Because individuals' objectives are relatively clear, whereas those of organizations are not, it is useful to define *all* economic property rights as rights possessed by individuals. Ultimately individuals always interact with other individuals, regardless of whether one or both interacting parties represent organizations in some capacity. The payments supermarket shoppers make for merchandise can be viewed as exchanges between individuals and an organization – between customers and the store. Such relationships, however, can always be reduced to the individual level. Let us consider the relationship between the cashier and the customers, on the one hand, and between the cashier and the store manager, on the other. A cashier in a store has the right to collect money from customers who buy merchandise in the store. The cashier, of course, does not usually retain customers' payments; rather, in exchange for an hourly wage, the cashier cedes to the store manager rights over his or her time as well as rights over the cash received from customers. In turn, the manager's relationships with other individuals such as the store owners involve other sets of exchanged rights. As I will demonstrate throughout this book, the functioning of any organization can be similarly reduced to the ceding of various rights from one individual associated with it to another.

The assumption of individual maximization and, in particular, the assumption that individuals maximize the value of their economic rights are useful not only directly in the analysis of individuals' behavior but also indirectly as the assumption underlying the functioning of organizations – indeed, of all societies. Individual maximization implies that whenever individuals perceive that certain actions will enhance the value of their rights, they will undertake such actions. This always applies, whether the individuals operate in markets, firms, families, tribes, government, or any other organization.

OPERATIONAL FEATURES OF
THE PROPERTY RIGHTS MODEL

The exchange value of an asset is a function of the gross income it can generate and of the costs of measuring and policing its exchange. The ownership of assets' attributes is expected to gravitate into the hands of those people who are most inclined to affect the income flow the attributes can generate. The gross income stream (the market value of the flow of services) an asset can generate, the value of the contributions of different individuals, and the costs of policing and measuring the attributes of the asset determine both how strictly rights to it will be delineated and what its ownership pattern will be. Since these and similar magnitudes are measurable, the ingredients necessary for an operational theory of property rights are available. These operational features also apply to the analysis of constraints.

Because of the costliness of delineating and policing rights, opportunities arise for some people to capture what appears to be others' wealth. As will be demonstrated in Chapter 3, these opportunities arise from people's ability to overuse and to underprovide unpriced attributes when exchanging with each other. Exchange partners may impose restrictions on one another in order to reduce the level of undesired behavior. Consequently, property rights – particularly the right to consume what appears to be one's own property – are often made subject to constraint. The character and incidence of the constraints are predictable. The analysis of constraints, therefore, can be incorporated into the study of property rights.

THE PROPERTY RIGHTS APPROACH VERSUS THE WALRASIAN MODEL

The presence of positive transaction costs is what makes the study of property rights significant. On the other hand, in the Walrasian, perfectly competitive model, rights are perfectly delineated and transaction costs are zero. It is useful, then, to briefly contrast the two models. A fundamental difference between the two concerns the role of prices. In the Walrasian model, costlessly determined prices suffice for all allocation problems. When transacting is costly, on the other hand, exchange requires non-price allocation methods with corresponding organizations.

In the Walrasian model, when equilibrium is disturbed a new equilibrium is instantaneously attained because, given zero transaction costs, the cost of adjustment is zero. In addition, Walrasian commodities are made up of strictly identical specimens, people are fully informed regarding the exchanged commodities, the terms of trade are always perfectly clear, and trade is instantaneous. As a result, neither buyer nor seller has to make any effort to incur any cost other than for the buyer to dispense the appropriate amount of cash and for the seller to cede the appropriate units of the good. Prices alone always *suffice* to allocate resources to their highest-value uses.

In the Walrasian model, where prices are sufficient for efficient allocation, institutions are superfluous; firms, clubs, tribes, or families cannot enhance efficiency. Nevertheless, for a long time economists attempted to address questions of organization by what amounted to ad hoc tinkering with the Walrasian model. Only recently have economists (and other social scientists) begun to take notice of the inconsistencies intrinsic to such an approach. The model used here explicitly explores the effects of positive information cost and the resulting positive transaction cost on behavior and on organization.

When equilibrium is disturbed in a positive transaction cost world, price adjustment is not expected to be instantaneous. As long as prices are not fully adjusted to new conditions, the quantities demanded are not, in general, equal to those supplied. Nevertheless, it is possible to determine how equilibrium will be attained. Where transaction costs are positive, a whole array of activities is required to effect exchange; cash with which to pay the pecuniary price is helpful but definitely not sufficient. Because of the complexity of exchange, parties have many opportunities to alter their behavior in order to gain from the discrepancy between the price actually charged and the one that would have achieved equilibrium.

To illustrate, consider some of the activities required to effect purchases in stores. Buyers must decide, among other things, whether to shop during the busiest hours (when, at the going price, the quantity demanded exceeds that supplied), or at off-peak times (when the reverse is true). They must then obtain all sorts of information: identify the location of the desired merchandise; determine by themselves or with the help of the sellers if the items they seek are available; decide if they are of the appropriate quality; select the specimens they think are best; ascertain the price, over which they may haggle; and make payment, not necessarily in cash. In addition, they may have to take care of warranties and, on occasion, exchange the merchandise. Completing purchases, then, involves an elaborate set of operations. More important, the costs and valuations of most of these operations can be altered. For instance, at any particular time a buyer may exercise return privileges more vigorously, and a seller may be out of an item that is usually in plentiful supply, or may unexpectedly help carry the merchandise to customers' cars. When the market-clearing price changes but the nominal price does not, buyers and sellers may still adjust in many ways. They can gain from such adjustments, and wealth maximization implies that adjustments will be forthcoming.

Sellers can adjust to a price that is lower than the market-clearing level along various margins. A seller who is in control of the quality of the merchandise or of the number of cashiers per customer will adjust along such margins, especially the latter. For example, supermarkets tend to reduce the speed of service at rush hours. In general, sellers who choose not to adjust prices or who are prevented from adjusting them may still adjust along other margins. Given wealth maximization, the margins along which they will adjust and the corresponding effects on resource allocation are predictable.

The analysis of non-price adjustments or of property rights need not be restricted to the market sector in an economy or to market economies;

on the contrary, the results of such analysis apply everywhere. They are as applicable to Hong Kong as they are to China during the Red Guard era or to tribes entirely without a market system. Application, of course, requires knowledge of the underlying constraints, and such knowledge may be harder to come by in some systems than in others. Although property rights analysis is usually applied to the capitalist market system only, it is most useful (and the Walrasian model is least useful) in systems in which market prices are least used and allowed to adjust. In Chapter 9 I will discuss briefly how property rights tools may be applied to a non-price economy.

Virtually all governments play a major role with regard to property rights; they also maintain the legal right to various properties and participate directly in economic activities. In addition, governments are heavily involved with adjudicating and enforcing contracts. A comprehensive analysis of the roles of government is beyond the scope of the present study; these roles will be touched on in Chapter 10 in the course of analyzing the behavior of individuals and enterprises.

Customs and mores seem to be additional non-price factors that affect the allocation of resources. However, the effects of these factors on behavior and on the enforcement of contracts will be ignored; although the factors to be considered are allowed to change, customs and mores, like tastes, are assumed to be stable and accordingly have no effect on the margin.

THE DISTINCTIVENESS OF THE PROPERTY RIGHTS APPROACH

An enormous amount of literature written in the last quarter century departs from the Walrasian, costless transacting, model. This literature, in which the costs of information play a major role, is diverse, and thus far no single model has stood out as the most useful one.[9] Different approaches with a bewildering array of names proliferate: "agency theory," or the "principal-agent model"; "market signaling"; "rent seeking"; "bounded rationality"; "asymmetric information"; and "contract theory." It is difficult to determine the precise differences between and even within these approaches because, as a rule, many assumptions are only implicit. Moreover, the empirical work in the area is too meager to help distinguish among them.

I shall not attempt to sort out these models, instead offering a few suggestions as to why I find such models to be less appealing than the property rights model. It should be made clear, though, that the

[9]Eggertsson (1990) elaborates on this point.

differences among the models often seem more a matter of emphasis than a reflection of different fundamental assumptions.

The starting point of "agency theory" is that principals' maximizing attempts are frustrated by agents whose objectives do not coincide with their own.[10] The asserted asymmetry between the two parties is likely to divert attention from the reciprocity of – and perhaps even from the gains deriving from – exchange. The "rent seeking" approach, whether applied to market or government activity, tends to ignore (almost to a fault) gains from exchange; it concentrates on people's efforts to capture wealth from each other and neglects the opportunities to gain through avoiding waste.[11] Indeed, it neglects the possibility that, individually *and* collectively, people take advantage of the opportunities available to avoid waste. In the process, they tend to exhaust these opportunities, and the cost of any further attempt must exceed the gain.

The problems inherent in the models based on asset specificity and on the opportunistic capture of quasi rent are very different.[12] Such models usually deal with variables that are exceedingly difficult to observe and to measure. The proxies required to make such models operational are even further removed from the desired variables than is usually the case in economics. Thus, it is particularly difficult to determine precisely what it is that empirical tests confirm or refute. "Market signaling," like rent seeking, emphasizes exploitation rather than maximization;[13] as with the asset specificity model, it is difficult to formulate empirical counterparts to the variables the theory suggests.

In contrast, contracts that use the state's assistance to delineate and reassign ownership are central to the property rights approach. The study of contracts formed by maximizing individuals, and of the performance such contracts induce, tends to reveal the correspondence between theoretical variables and their empirical counterparts. Knight (1924) was apparently the first to specifically point out the economic role of property rights, and Gordon's (1954) thrust is similar. Coase (1960), Alchian (1965), and Cheung (1969) bring operational elements to the analysis. I wish to emphasize an additional element that helps keep reality in touch: a constant inquiry as to "who owns what" and what, precisely, it is that each party receives and concedes in a transaction. These simple points are nevertheless worth mentioning because they are frequently over-

[10] Ross (1973) and Jensen and Meckling (1976) are early proponents of agency theory.
[11] Tullock (1967), Krueger (1974), and Posner (1975) initiated the rent-seeking literature.
[12] Williamson (1975) and Klein, Crawford, and Alchian (1978) initiated the notion of the capture of quasi rent.
[13] This approach had been initiated by Arrow (1973) and Spence (1973).

looked. The relative ease of rendering the property rights model operational will be made clear in the following chapters.[14]

The property rights model developed in Chapters 3, 4, and 5 will be used to follow through on Demsetz's (1967) and Umbeck's (1977) embryonic contributions to rights formation. In Chapter 6 I shall try to show that the property rights model is useful in predicting when new rights will be created and when existing rights will be placed in the public domain. I shall also argue that such changes pervade economic activity.[15] Several empirical tests of property rights propositions involving such diverse activities as slavery, the allocation of water rights in the western United States, and the homestead movement will be presented in the following chapters.

[14] Akerlof, in his pioneering study (1970), recognizes the effect of the non-uniformity of commodities and of the inadequacy of the received model of handling them.
[15] Another distinction of my study – although this need not be unique to the property rights approach – is that I take no account of problems of risk aversion; all my attempts to explain behavior proceed under the assumption of risk neutrality. As I will demonstrate in Chapter 3, there is much to be gained and little to be lost by assuming people to be risk-neutral.

2

The public domain:
Rationing by waiting and price controls

In the following discussion an elaboration of a single example – the gasoline price controls of the 1970s – serves to illustrate the usefulness and power of the property rights framework. It also introduces tools that are useful in analyzing situations not subject to government intervention, in which the price of a commodity (or a commodity-attribute) differs from the (supposed) market clearing price.

Chapter 1 presented a property rights proposition central to this book: Given that property rights are never perfectly delineated, some valued properties will always be in the public domain. In the present chapter the nature of maximization, as affected by properties in the public domain, will be examined and the actual resolutions of several public domain issues will be analyzed. Because an analysis of rationing by waiting offers a convenient introduction to the subject of property rights, I will briefly concentrate on such an analysis; subsequent discussion will provide a more detailed analysis of maximization under price controls, which will highlight major features of the substance and the mechanics of property rights.

RATIONING BY WAITING

The rationing by waiting model used here, which is stripped of many real-world features, is most elementary. Using this model makes it easy to concentrate on the public domain issue while ignoring peripheral problems. I will use the results of this basic analysis in my subsequent analysis of the price controls placed on gasoline in the early 1970s.

When the government provides commodities at a zero pecuniary price and makes them available on a first-come, first-served basis, which it enforces, commodities are allocated strictly according to the order in which individuals join the queue, and ultimately by the amount of time individuals spend waiting in line. Even though orderly queues are often encountered, they should not be taken for granted, as the following example illustrates. Suppose it is *publicly announced* that a package containing a million dollars is to be given to the first person in line at a particular place. It might seem that anyone who hears the announcement would rush to be the first at the site and wait for the package to arrive. If, however, the line is not to be policed, the ultimate owner of the money is likely to be someone with an armored truck and a machine gun. In the absence of policing, those who hear such an announcement will probably not bother to join the queue unless they are able to compete effectively with owners of machine guns.

Competition for the free good may take a variety of forms. The specific nature of restrictions delineates the margins of competition. In the previous example, the restrictions are first-come, first-served and no policing, whereas in the current example the margins are firepower rather than time. Other margins are used in other cases. For instance, higher education is often provided free or for a low monetary fee, and the margin of competition for admission is a combination of residency and grade requirements. The provider of the free good may stipulate first-come, first-served; the queue will be orderly provided the appropriate restrictions are applied. Such restrictions seem to be applied often, and orderly rationing by waiting is a common occurrence. In the discussion that follows I assume that the queue is policed so that it remains orderly.

The price-setting mechanics developed in price-theory texts can be used to determine the properties of the first-come, first-served allocation. On the supply side, the government furnishes a fixed quantity of a good. I will make a single change from the textbook mechanics on the demand side: consumers exchange commodities for time rather than for money. Given the fixed supply, forces of demand determine the equilibrium price per unit of the good being distributed in terms of the amount of time spent by individuals in the queue. Almost anything that can be said about money in the standard case applies to time when allocation is determined by waiting.[1]

One evident and important difference between rationing by dollars and rationing by time, however, is that allotment of dollars across individuals differs from the corresponding allotment of time. If waiting time per unit of a good is five minutes, waiting is the only method of acquiring the good, and if the good cannot be traded, then a person will stand in line to obtain additional units of the good until the value of five minutes of his time reaches the value of one extra unit. For example, when the value of the individual's time is $12 per hour (or $1 for five minutes), he will continue to rejoin the line to obtain another unit of the good as long

---

[1] See Barzel 1974, pp. 73–95.

as his marginal valuation of the good exceeds $1. If the price of the good becomes $1 instead of five minutes, the analysis proceeds along standard lines. Given that the good cannot be traded, however, the inframarginal individuals who ultimately get the good are those who value it most in time rather than in money.

Changes in the rules governing the distribution of the good can be accommodated easily according to this model of rationing by waiting. For instance, there is no reason to assume that the given commodity will be doled out in fixed batches. There are other possible rules governing its distribution: individuals may be allowed as much of it as they desire; access to the line may be limited to once per period or to an unlimited number of times; and once the commodity is obtained, trading it may be permitted. Each rule constitutes a distinct way of allocating rights to the good.

This basic analysis of rationing by waiting yields one key result: A commodity announced to be free is effectively placed in the public domain and is of no value until ownership is established. Establishing ownership requires that an individual fulfill certain criteria; in the present example, the criterion is to spend five minutes in a queue. Acquisition of the commodity consumes real resources over and above the resources used in production. In this example, ownership is established over one already produced unit of the commodity. Methods differ from case to case, but whatever the method by which rights are acquired, it may generally be stated that resources must be spent to gain possession of commodities in the public domain, that individual maximization applies here no less than to conventional exchange, and that persons who have a comparative advantage in the method of allocation will acquire the good.

PRICE CONTROL ANALYSIS

How are property rights allocated to a commodity that is sold at a price below the market equilibrium level? In the model of rationing by waiting, queuing is the means by which ownership is established. Rationing by waiting can be viewed as a special case of price control.

Real-world price controls differ from rationing by waiting in two important ways. First, whereas the analysis of price control requires only that the controlled price be lower than the equilibrium price, in the rationing by waiting model I assume that the (money) price is zero.[2] Second, whereas in the rationing by waiting model I assume that competition can occur only through queuing, in the price control analysis that assumption is maintained only initially.

[2] I focus on below-equilibrium price controls (i.e., price ceilings) and ignore above-equilibrium price controls (i.e., price floors).

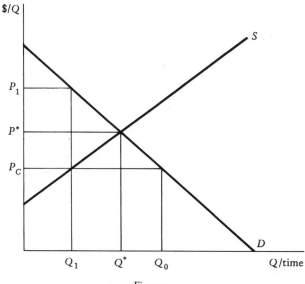

Figure 2.1

In the rationing by waiting model, individuals acquire rights to the rationed commodity by spending the appropriate amount of time in the queue. Under price controls, rights allocation is more complex, and the determination of how rights to an asset are actually allocated is essential for the analysis of the controls.[3] In the remainder of this chapter I will analyze the price controls that were placed on gasoline in the early 1970s. Before undertaking this analysis, however, it is worthwhile to look at a generic price control model.

In the generic model, it is assumed that competition initially emerges as queuing. Consider Figure 2.1, where D is the demand curve, S is the supply curve, the equilibrium price and quantity are P^* and Q^*, and the control price is P_C. Assuming that the control price is perfectly enforced, a discrepancy between quantity demanded, Q_0, and quantity supplied, Q_1, known as a "shortage," will arise. Sellers will supply only Q_1; Q_1 then, is the quantity available to consumers, a quantity for which they will be willing to pay P_1.

In considering the effects of the price control on resource allocation, it should be restated that in the Walrasian model, in the absence of government regulations, rights are well defined and allocation is efficient. Had a tax of $(P_1 - P_C)$ been imposed, the market quantity would have also been Q_1. The standard analysis of the welfare, or deadweight loss, from

[3] See Cheung 1974, pp. 53–71.

such a tax is that it equals the triangle between the demand and supply curves to the right of Q_1; the excess of the amount consumers are willing to pay over the resource cost of producing the quantity $(Q^* - Q_1)$ which is not produced because of the tax. This is sometimes also asserted to be the deadweight loss from controlling the price at P_C; as the rationing by waiting discussion suggests, this is not the case.

Because consumers can pay only P_C in money, they will spend resources equivalent to the difference $(P_1 - P_C)$ by waiting in line. For example, if $Q_1 = 100$, $P_C = 1$, $P_1 = \$1.80$, and the opportunity cost for consumers is $10 per hour, then buyers in the aggregate will spend a total of $100 in money and eight hours in time to purchase one hundred units. The amount represented by the area $P_1 - P_C \times Q_1$ is the dollar value of the time expenditure. Because queuing is the only margin of competition, this is the new equilibrium under the price control. As the discussion proceeds, various simplifying assumptions underlying the generic model will be dropped. It is essential, however, to describe the control itself and its background.

The Economic Stabilization Act of 1970 gave the president of the United States the authority to impose controls on prices. On August 15, 1971, President Richard Nixon imposed a ninety-day economywide freeze of all prices at their May 1971 level. This freeze was known as Phase I of the price control and was succeeded by several more phases, each involving some voluntary and some mandatory controls.[4] The final one, Phase IV, lasted into 1974 and was essentially a period of gradual price deregulation.

For many commodities the price controls caused inconveniences: Fewer sales were made on credit, a smaller variety of goods was available, and free delivery was less frequent. As a rule, however, shortages did not arise. In the case of gasoline, the discrepancy between the controlled price and the market-clearing price that would have prevailed without the controls was too large to mask some of the effects of the price controls.[5] In the wake of the eruption of the Arab–Israeli war on October 6, 1973, the Organization of Petroleum Exporting Countries (OPEC) restricted exports and raised the price of crude petroleum. Prior to the war, the world price of crude oil had been around $3 a barrel. On

---

[4] Much of the information on the Nixon administration price controls comes from Kalt (1981) and Rockoff (1984). In the case of retail gasoline, prices were not explicitly controlled; instead, the margins, or markups, were controlled at various stages. Only the price of crude petroleum was controlled. (This information was provided by Bruce Peterson of the American Petroleum Institute and Del Fogelquist of the Western Oil and Gas Association.) The Cost of Living Council and the Internal Revenue Service were the primary agencies involved in policing and enforcement of the controls.

[5] The meaning of "too large" is clarified in the last paragraph of the section entitled "The Minimization of Dissipation" in this chapter.

October 16 OPEC raised the price to nearly $5 a barrel, and on December 23 the price was raised to $11.56 per barrel.[6] This drastic price increase – more than threefold – coupled with price control led to shortages and queuing in the United States by December 1973. Some aspects of these shortages may conveniently be analyzed using the property rights model.

The gasoline transaction

The purchase of gasoline may appear to be a simple operation. In the course of this chapter, however, it should become clear that gasoline transactions have numerous valued attributes. During the period of price controls, market participants were able to alter the levels of gasoline-transaction attributes not controlled by the government. For that reason the actual allocation of property rights differed from what the nominal controls seemed to specify. An examination of this price control episode reveals the strength of the property rights framework by responding to the question of how individuals were able to benefit from the use or exchange of commodities under the controls. It also suggests areas for economic inquiry and is helpful in developing refutable implications.

Figure 2.2 shows the change in circumstances in the gasoline market induced by the Arab–Israeli war of 1973. In May 1971 the price of regular gasoline was about 35 cents per gallon (P_C). The crude-oil price hike that resulted from the war caused a shift up and to the left in the supply of gasoline, from something like $S_{May\ 1971}$ to $S_{Dec.\ 1973}$, as depicted in Figure 2.2.[7] In the absence of price controls, P^*, the market-clearing price would have been around 55 cents per gallon after this decline in supply.[8]

What effect did price controls have on the behavior of market participants? Prior to Cheung's work, the price control literature asserted that a shortage of $(Q_0 - Q_1)$ would arise, that the typical consumer would acquire a fraction of the amount of gasoline desired.[9] One also encounters in the literature the contentions that the shortage would be borne proportionately, randomly, or arbitrarily. Such contentions are without foundation. The Walrasian framework provides no guidance regarding behavior under the indicated conditions, although random allocation

---

[6] The average per-barrel regulated price of crude oil in the United States was $3.89 for 1973 and $6.87 for 1974. See *Statistical Abstract of the United States 1986*, p. 698.

[7] Control of the wholesale price of gasoline complicates but does not change the essence of the analysis.

[8] As controls were relinquished, the uncontrolled price of gasoline finally leveled off at around 55 cents per gallon in the summer of 1974.

[9] Cheung (1974) provides a review of this literature.

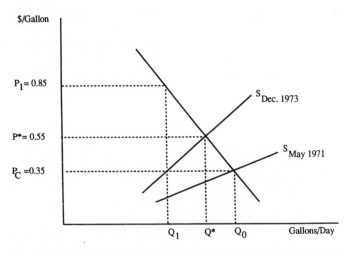

Figure 2.2

seems to be the most likely result from extending that framework.[10] The view adopted here asserts that in reality people have many margins of action that the Walrasian model abstracts from. Given these margins of action, wealth maximization will generate a determinate equilibrium.

Wealth maximization implies that individuals will carry on an activity until (for the marginal unit) net gains are zero. Even when a price is controlled, the question must be asked: Can the buyer or the seller take additional steps to obtain or provide another unit at a cost below the added gain? If the answer is yes, an equilibrium has not yet been reached. The notion of a "market-clearing" equilibrium requires that all individuals make whatever moves they wish under the existing property rights arrangement. The textbook analysis of a binding price ceiling that concludes that a shortage will emerge implicitly assumes that buyers pay in cash and that they receive the right amount of the right quality of the commodity at the right time and place. It ignores the possibility of adjustments, thus implicitly denying that individuals maximize if adjustments are available. The way in which margins of adjustment were exploited under the gasoline price controls will be examined in the following section.

[10] If the Q_1 available units are allocated randomly among the demanders of the Q_0 units, then the deadweight loss is not the conventional welfare triangle. Rather, it is proportionate to the entire area under the demand curve above P_C (up to quantity Q_0), the factor of proportionality being $(Q_0 - Q_1)/Q_1$.

The public domain

Preliminary considerations of property rights under the controls

The Nixon administration could have exercised several options instead of – or in addition to – simply imposing price controls. For instance, it could have required producers to continue to produce the quantity Q^* or, for that matter, the quantity Q_0. No quantity restrictions were imposed, however. On the demand side, as the shortage became severe, the administration could have estimated Q_1 (see Figure 2.2) and issued coupons for that number of gallons. Had coupons been issued, rights to the purchase of gasoline would have been allocated. Property rights would then have been secure and people would not have needed to spend resources to acquire these rights. Coupons, however, were not issued. What property rights system prevailed under the price control?

Earlier, in connection with Figure 2.1, I made the general statement that when the maximum price for a commodity is set at P_C, the quantity of it that will be available in the marketplace is Q_1. Underlying this statement are two important assumptions about property rights, one explicit and the other implicit. The explicit assumption is that under price controls the sellers' right to set prices is restricted; here sellers of gasoline were legally prohibited from selling it at any price above 35 cents per gallon. The implicit assumption is that sellers retain the right to provide whatever quantity they wish. Given the sellers' marginal cost curve and the control price of 35 cents per gallon, the maximizing quantity they would have offered was Q_1, as indicated in Figure 2.2.

Consumers wished to purchase Q_0 at the control price, but this quantity had no operational relevance: None of the forces under the control depended on this quantity. Q_1 was ultimately the quantity that was allocated among the consumers. P_1 is the maximum price that consumers would pay to purchase the (entire) quantity Q_1, which in Figure 2.2 is 85 cents per gallon of gasoline. Q_1, the quantity offered at P_C, was the quantity that consumers wanted to purchase at the higher price P_1. In reality rationing by waiting turned out to be the equilibrating force, given that the maximum price sellers had the right to charge was lower than the one buyers were willing to pay.

Rationing of gasoline by waiting

Why did waiting lines for gasoline materialize in the fall of 1973? Shortages per se are not a cause for waiting. Indeed, scarcity does not imply "shortage"; in December 1973, at 55 cents per gallon there would have been no shortage of gasoline. The quantity supplied would have declined from Q_0 in May 1971 to Q^* in December 1973, Q^* being the quantity demanded at that price. Gasoline, of course, was "scarce." A commodity is scarce if something has to be sacrificed to obtain it. Since 50 cents per gallon had to be sacrificed to obtain gasoline, it must have been scarce. The appearance of a shortage arose because the price was controlled at a level below the market-clearing price. It was noted earlier that there are many ways to resolve a shortage; waiting is just one of these. Waiting lines did emerge late in 1973. It is curious that the regulators never formally adopted queuing as the method of allocating gasoline. It became clear, however, that although it was subject to various exceptions and added controls, this was the only method of distribution that the regulator was going to allow.

Under the price control, the actual pecuniary price per gallon of gasoline was positive – 35 cents. Rationing by waiting was analyzed on the assumption that the pecuniary price is zero, but as long as the controlled price of gasoline is held below the market-clearing price, the queuing analysis essentially applies. Something valued by consumers and initially owned by sellers was not charged for; thus gasoline was partially placed in the public domain, and the queue served to establish rights over the unowned component. Gasoline sellers owned the property rights to 35 cents per gallon of gasoline, and buyers could acquire rights to the difference between P_1 and P_C – which in Figure 2.2 is 50 cents per gallon – by joining the queue. If the wage rate of the marginal waiter had been $6 per hour (or 10 cents per minute), the market-clearing queue length would have been five minutes per gallon.[11]

Given that buyers acquired gasoline by a combined expenditure of money and time, the conventional demand curve is somewhat misspecified. As it is usually formulated, it shows the maximum amount of money people will pay for varying amounts of gasoline when no waiting is required, but not how much they will pay in terms of a combination of money and time. It is easy to construct a modified demand curve in which the price is stated in minutes per gallon, given that 35 cents per gallon

---

[11] An important complication arises with regard to the mechanics of the queue. It makes a difference if gasoline is rationed by the gallon or by the tank. In most cases gasoline was rationed by the (capacity of the) tank. A person who drove a car with a small tank could get less gasoline for each waiting episode than someone whose car had a large tank. Since waiting time was independent of the size of the gas tank, savings associated with purchase size became more prominent.

According to the present model, running out of gas was *not* the result of the price control. By waiting in line and then paying 35 cents a gallon, one could always get gasoline. Independent of shortages, a person can save resources (time) by filling the tank less often, and people occasionally do run out of gas by postponing purchase too long. Under price controls, the expectations are, first, that people will run out of gas more often and, second, that among automobiles running out of gas, relatively more prevalent will be those with a small driving range (per full tank). For these cars, the increase in the per-gallon cost of filling the tank is higher.

must also be paid. Such a demand curve displays marginal valuation in terms of time per unit over and above 35 cents per unit. This type of demand curve depends not only on the valuation of gasoline but also on the opportunity cost of time. Of two individuals who have identical demands for gasoline but who differ in their opportunity cost of time, the one with the low opportunity cost will outbid the other once waiting becomes part of the price of gasoline. In the discussion that follows, demand is assumed to account for the two components of price.

To return to the main issue, the price control reassigned the rights of sellers and buyers to gasoline. The sellers had the right to the value of the gasoline up to the control price, and the remainder was placed in the public domain. Buyers could acquire the right to the remainder – the difference between the control price and the buyers' marginal valuation – by joining a queue. By paying the control price plus the time price, buyers could obtain the property rights to a gallon of gasoline. Except for the fact that buyers had to pay a pair of prices, the market for gasoline may be viewed as having functioned normally. Indeed, there are many unregulated markets in which both money and time prices are paid by the buyer. A person who insists on eating lunch at noon in the cafeteria is charged a money price by the cashier while facing a time price as well, namely, waiting time. In this case the pecuniary price is fixed by the seller. In the case of gasoline the money price was fixed by government.[12]

What are the regulators regulating?

The preceding analysis contains many implicit assumptions that connect the waiting price with the control price. In the next few sections some of these assumptions will be altered in order to increase the correspondence between the waiting model and the actual situation.

The approximate average price of gasoline in the United States in May 1971 was 35 cents per gallon. In the analysis, a single control price of 35 cents per gallon was used. The gasoline price control stipulated, however, that the maximum price a station could charge was the *actual* price it charged in May 1971. These prices were subject to considerable variation. Prices were lower at gas stations in oil-producing states, reflecting lower transportation costs. Prices were higher for premium than for regular gasoline. Prices were lower at gas stations that used low prices as promotional devices than at gas stations that used other means of promotion. Prices were lower at self-service stations. A self-service station selling regular gasoline at 34 cents per gallon in the summer of 1973 would

---

[12] Deacon and Sonstelie (1985) exploit a gasoline price-control episode in the aftermath of the 1973–4 era. They successfully test some of the hypotheses suggested here, as well as some related ones.

have had to sell regular gasoline at a maximum price of 34 cents during the price control, and a full-service station selling regular at 38 cents during this period would have had its maximum price fixed at 38 cents. A price control constitutes the assignment of property rights; assuming that the regulators could easily ascertain the actual base price and could easily enforce it, delineation was clear in one important respect: Each seller knew exactly what price he or she could legally charge.[13] In other essential respects, however, delineation was less clear.

What, exactly, is it that one purchases in a gas station? "Gasoline" is not a sufficient answer. The buyer is expected to optimize regarding such things as purchase frequency and to get gasoline at the lowest net resource cost for a given quality service. Like all transacted commodities, gasoline has a large number of valuable attributes. For example, when is it available? Is the gas station open nine or twenty-four hours per day? Is the octane rating 88 or 98? Is the station self- or full-service? In addition, the costliness of the transaction includes travel and search time as well as time in the station. It is essential to have specific information about the regulation of the attributes of gasoline before its effects can be adequately examined. Ambiguity surrounded the regulation of such attributes under price controls.

Much of the ambiguity in the scope of controls stems from the great number and variability of attributes of gasoline. The attributes of gasoline transactions can be classified into those of the gasoline itself and those of the services provided with the gasoline. One of the attributes of the gasoline itself is its octane rating. Gasoline is commonly graded as regular or premium, depending on that rating.[14] Hence "premium gasoline" describes a range of products of octane 90 and above, rather than strictly defining a single product. (I assume, more or less in conformity with actual practice, that under the price control premium gasoline had to have a minimum octane rating of 90.) There are other variations among premium gasolines. For example, Exxon's premium gasoline had performance additives different from Shell's, and the premium gasoline sold in the Rocky Mountains was refined differently from that sold at sea-level locations. The price control essentially ignored most of the variations in gasoline quality. Because it is prohibitively costly to delineate rights to all the valuable attributes of a commodity, it is not surprising that the control specifications were not fully detailed. Correspondingly,

---

[13] Actually, it is difficult to ascertain precisely the price used by the regulators.

[14] Premium and regular grades are generally determined by industry standards through the American Petroleum Institute (API) and the American Society for Testing and Methods (ASTM). Bruce Peterson of the API reports that the standards are voluntary, although there are some state regulations, with varying degrees of enforcement. No single octane rating is specified to distinguish regular from premium.

it is expected that regulations also consistently fail to specifically stipulate the level of certain attributes. Indeed, the real-world price control specified only the grade of gasoline and largely ignored other attributes, including the service provided.

In my initial analysis, in which gasoline was implicitly considered as a homogeneous commodity, it was seen that price controls effectively allowed the seller to retain the right to 35 cents per gallon and allowed buyers to capture the remaining value (which had been placed in the public domain) by joining a queue. This conclusion must be reexamined in light of the opportunity sellers had to adjust the quality of their gasoline. Although it set prices according to May 1971 standards, the regulation did not require sellers to match the precise quality of gasoline they had sold during this period. With product quality as a variable, and with a regulation that did not specify all of the relevant attributes, property rights had become extremely murky by late 1971.

When attributes subject to variability are incompletely specified, the affected parties correspondingly have some leeway, each according to her particular circumstances. To illustrate, consider two stations, A and B, which were selling premium gasoline in the spring of 1971. Station A sold 90-octane premium for 39 cents per gallon, and station B sold 92-octane premium for 41 cents. As stated, when the price control was imposed, the lowest octane level at which a gasoline was still considered premium was 90. Station A was restricted to a maximum price of 39 cents per gallon and to a minimum octane level of 90, thus requiring it to maintain its octane at the old level. Station B was restricted to a maximum price of 41 cents per gallon but to a minimum octane level of 90. Station B could thus lower its octane to below the pre-control levels while continuing to sell the gasoline as premium and to charge 41 cents per gallon for it. If gas stations had to pay refiners 1 cent per gallon for each unit increase in octane level, Station B was able to save 2 cents per gallon of premium gasoline.

As long as consumers were willing to pay more than 41 cents per gallon for premium gasoline (i.e., $P_1 > 0.41$), they were willing to pay the higher money price for B's gasoline, provided that the time price they had to pay was correspondingly less than for A's gasoline. Since the time price was spent to acquire rights from the public domain and was not transferred to anyone, there was no countervailing loss from the reduction in waiting time when buying B's higher-price gasoline. The government's specification of rights played into the hands of Station B. By adjusting gasoline quality without violating the regulation, it could capture some of the value of the gasoline that seemed to end up in the public domain as a result of the price control.

The preceding analysis is based on some major property rights propositions. The logical derivation may be correct, but there is no a priori reason to accept the model that generated the preceding conclusions as a good description of reality. This must be determined empirically. Whereas no actual empirical investigation was conducted, the following three tests are capable of refuting the preceding analysis. First, gasoline quality in terms of octane levels should have declined as sellers attempted to capture the value that was placed in the public domain. More specifically, the per-gallon amount of the refining additive tetra-ethyl-lead used to boost the octane level should have declined. Second, the quantity of antiknock additives (i.e., substitutes for octane sold separately from gasoline) should have increased subsequent to the imposition of the price control. Third, waiting time in the higher-price stations should have been lower than in the lower-price stations; moreover, buyers in the higher-price stations should have placed a greater value on their time than did buyers in the lower-price stations. The results of these tests would be a good indication of the credibility of the hypotheses generated by the model.

An analysis similar to that of the octane level applies to other attributes of the gasoline itself as well as to the gas station services. No matter what specifications the regulator stipulated, whether explicit or implicit, the suppliers could increase their profit by just meeting them, provided that before the controls were imposed these specifications were exceeded. Here, too, the reduction in quality of the product did not harm consumers, who simply spent fewer resources on acquiring the less-valued rights that were placed in the public domain.

Turning to gas station services, the type and level of services attached to the purchase of gasoline vary considerably from station to station. As it applied to gasoline, the price control regulation specified nothing about the level of services to be provided along with the gasoline. The response in this case is expected to have been similar to that of the octane levels. A simple scenario of two stations that differ only in terms of the level of services provided can isolate the effects of this lack of specification. Station C sells regular gasoline for 33 cents per gallon and provides few extra services.[15] Station D sells the same regular gasoline for 36 cents but provides 3 cents' worth of services per gallon in the form of pumping the gas, cleaning the windshield, and looking under the hood. Once the price control is imposed, Station C can charge no more than 33 cents per gallon, while Station D can charge no more than 36 cents. Station D, like Station B in the previous example, has an additional margin of adjust-

[15] Convenient locations and smoothly functioning pumps are examples of services even low-service gas stations still provided. Under competition in general, if a station was selling gasoline at a price higher than what it had paid for it (including transportation), some extra service must have been provided.

ment not available to Station C. Station D can reduce its service level to zero, thereby saving 3 cents per gallon in costs, and still sell gasoline for 36 cents, which enables it to avoid losing some of its wealth to the public domain. Consumers will buy all that station D can sell at 36 cents a gallon without service so long as the cost of waiting at station C exceeds 3 cents per gallon.

Gas station owners were able to alter still other margins of their product without violating the letter of the regulation. One of these margins was station hours. Station owners could choose their hours of operation, thereby lowering costs without violating the regulation. Selling gasoline is more costly in the middle of the night than during business hours because night workers must be paid a higher wage and security is more problematic. Perhaps because complex pricing schemes are costly to operate, twenty-four-hour stations charge the same price at all hours. The average cost of twenty-four–hour stations is higher than that of stations open only during daytime hours; the single price charged by the former must therefore be higher than that charged by the latter. The price control required stations not to exceed the old price but did not require them to keep their old hours. Most stations that had been open twenty-four hours a day quickly shortened their hours of service. Such stations were thus able to charge prices higher than those charged by others while incurring the same costs.[16]

The model here offers a prediction regarding gas station survival. The available supply of gasoline declined during the era of price controls, and the number of stations selling it also got smaller. Those stations that had the greatest number of margins at which to adjust are expected to have been able to tolerate the price control situation longer than those with fewer margins of adjustment. Because consumers were paying the same full price (i.e., time plus money) for the same product no matter where they made the purchase, they were unconcerned about paying a higher money price and waiting for less time at the first kind of station and doing the reverse at the second. Thus, self-service (or no-service) stations, being the ones having fewer margins at which to adjust to price controls, are expected to have been among the first to go out of business. Stations already selling premium at the lowest possible octane level before the price controls are expected to have been similarly affected. These implications are testable, although the data for the latter implication may be more difficult to collect.

Thus far I have considered only those margins of adjustment that were open to sellers. Other margins existed at which only buyers or both buyers and sellers could adjust in order to minimize dissipation. Resources

---

[16] Eventually most stations reduced their hours to the minimum number required to dispense their gasoline allocations.

spent in the queue were not received by others, and the existence of queues indicates that potential gains from sidestepping them existed. One common way to circumvent price controls, and thus to lower the losses therefrom, was to tie the sale of gasoline to the sale of another product not subject to price controls. Owners were able to use lubrication and other gas station services to mask the true price of gasoline to the regulators, who did allow for such ties. A customer whose waiting cost for a full tank of gasoline was $5 was willing to pay up to $5 above the competitive price of lubrication when it was offered with a full tank of gas and no waiting. The seller who provided such an offer was able to capture some of the value that had formerly been dissipated by waiting. At no previous time in history had automobiles been so well lubricated.

THE MINIMIZATION OF DISSIPATION

The analysis of adjustment by sellers regarding customer service is useful for bringing out an important point developed by Cheung. He recognized that price controls attenuate property rights and place some potential income in the public domain. Income is made non-exclusive, and resources are spent to capture it. An equally important point Cheung made is that the maximization hypothesis implies that the parties to the transaction will act so as to make the dissipation a constrained minimum. In the case considered here, by adjusting their levels of service downward as the constraint of price controls became binding, sellers were able to capture a value that would otherwise have been left in the public domain. This action is a component of the minimization of dissipation.

Consider the following example, illustrated in Figure 2.3. S_0 and D_0 are the supply and demand curves for full-service regular gasoline before the supply decrease and before the implementation of the price control, and P_C, 35 cents per gallon, is the market price. That price ultimately became the control price. The supply then shifted leftward to S_1, and P_C became the binding control price. Had sellers continued to offer full service, they would have supplied a quantity Q_1 for which consumers were willing to pay 85 cents per gallon. The difference between that price and the control price would have been dissipated in the form of time spent in the queue. The total value of the queuing dissipation is shown by the vertically shaded rectangle, representing an amount of 50 cents per gallon for Q_1 gallons. This 50 cents per gallon was lost in the sense that the customers' time expenditure was received by no one. As indicated, the seller could capture some of this dissipated income by reducing gasoline quality and services.

Because gasoline continued to be sold by the gallon, the coordinates of Figure 2.3 have the correct units for the changed product, while the supply

30

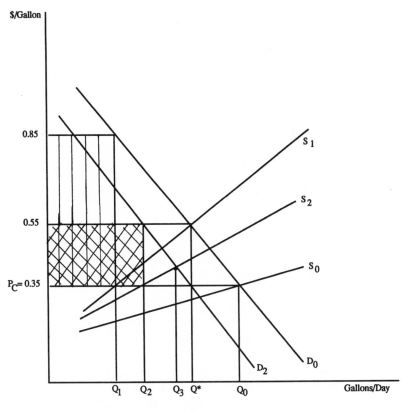

Figure 2.3

and demand curves for the new quality must be redrawn. S_2 is the new supply of gasoline, the production of which required fewer resources per gallon because of the elimination of services. Consumers' valuation of the no-service gasoline was less than that of full-service gasoline; D_2 is the new demand. The eliminated services, however, were valued by consumers more than they cost to produce; this is why they were provided to begin with. The intersection between the no-service curves S_2 and D_2 at quantity Q_3 must therefore be to the left of the intersection between D_0 and S_1 at quantity Q^*. The fall in quantity from Q^* to Q_3 is a reflection of a cost of regulation that the adjustments could not eliminate. The dissipation per gallon was reduced (to 20 cents in the example), and the number of gallons of gasoline (Q_2) was larger than in the absence of the adjustment (Q_1). The total dissipation after service reduction, which is shown by the crosshatched area (combined with the appropriate "welfare triangles"), is less than the dissipation without the service reduction.

Economic analysis of property rights

I stated earlier that before October 1973 the discrepancy between the market price and the control price was not "too large"; the meaning of the latter now becomes clear. Before October 1973 the adjustment in gasoline quality was sufficient to yield an equilibrium price as low as 35 cents per gallon; thus, no waiting lines emerged. Given the many margins available for adjustment, maximization here meant that various components of service such as windshield cleaning were eliminated. Elimination began at the lowest net value service and went up as the discrepancy between the control and the clearing price increased. After October 1973, the price control constraint in the gasoline market was so severe that even when sellers had taken advantage of all the available adjustments, the equilibrium price exceeded 35 cents a gallon. Consequently shortages ensued and queues were required to ration the available quantity.

CONCLUSION

The foregoing analysis of rationing by waiting and of price controls has shown that because of the complexity of transactions, market participants can adjust to many margins besides quantity and price. Maximization implies that such margins will be exploited, and the pattern of that exploitation is predictable: People will use the lowest-cost methods available to them under the constraints to reclaim the value that the regulations place in the public domain. As a result of such actions, dissipation from the regulations is minimized. In the case of the gasoline price controls of the 1970s, adjustments were made to provide the lowest permitted octane levels, the shortest possible hours of operation for service stations, and the very frequent lubrication of automobiles.

The analysis of a situation in which price is controlled by the government at a level below (or, for that matter, above) the market price applies quite generally to situations controlled purely by market forces as well. The similarity lies in the fact that, with the exception of organized markets such as the stock exchange, many market-controlled prices are kept constant in the face of constantly changing conditions. For instance, the price of coffee changes by the minute on the coffee futures exchange, and within supermarkets demand changes by the hour of the day and by the day of the week. The supermarket price, however, often stays unchanged for weeks. Therefore, not only price but other factors as well must affect the allocation. Waiting is just one such factor. The main difference between the analysis of the adjustment to government controlled prices and to unchanging market prices is the greater leeway sellers have over the criteria by which to allocate their commodities in the non-controlled situation.

32

3

Contract choice: The tenancy contract

At the heart of the study of property rights lies the study of contracts. Contracts, whether formal or informal, reallocate rights among contracting parties. I will focus here on private contracts that are enforceable by the courts and the police. The tenancy contract between tenant and landlord – between the owner of labor and the owner of land – is relatively simple and is thus a suitable point from which to begin the study of contracts.

On a family farm, a single operator or a single family – the owner of labor – undertakes the bulk of farm activities. Family farming is common and relatively simply organized. By studying tenancy contracts in the context of family farming, it is possible to isolate some basic contracting problems that may be obscured in more complex organizations.[1] As a background to the analysis of the tenancy contract I offer a critical review of the traditional approach to the relationship between tenant and landlord.

THE SHARE CONTRACT AND CHEUNG'S CONTRIBUTION

Price theory textbooks routinely introduce the notion of a production function and discuss the marginal product of a factor such as labor for given levels of such other factors as capital and land. Given the productivity of the factors and the market prices of factors and products, it is easy to determine both the optimum amounts and the values of the contributions of each factor. The assumptions that factors are uniform and that all relevant information is freely available usually underlie these

---

[1] Allen and Lueck (1992, 1993) have done extensive work on family farm contracts in the United States.

discussions. In such a setting, the problem of organizing production is trivial.

These textbook assumptions are violated in reality. Problems arise because efficient production requires that many owners of specialized, non-uniform productive inputs cooperate under conditions for which random factors also affect output. In agriculture, weather, pests, and other forces affect output differently during different periods and at different locations. In addition, no two pieces of land are identical, nor are any two workers. Determining the properties of each unit of input requires extensive and costly measurement. Owing to diversity in the forces that affect output, the specific contributions of individuals are extremely difficult to determine. Compensating factor-owners according to the average contribution is not satisfactory here, because individuals can mask their own low-level contributions by attributing them to other forces. Such attempts to capture wealth make cooperation among individuals costly. Individuals will organize their transactions to maximize the value of their output net of conventional input costs and of the wealth capture costs, the latter being part of the costs of transacting. As I shall explain, individuals can gain by organizing their transactions in such a way as to lower these costs.

The inefficiency associated with the share contract is a particular manifestation of the wealth-capture problem. Having been recognized long ago, it has received a great deal of attention from economists. In a share contract, a landlord lets a tenant work the land in exchange for a share of the output. The tenant's payment to the landlord may be likened to an ad valorem tax, and this analogy has been used to suggest that the share contract is inefficient.

Let me first consider briefly the ad valorem tax. The demand facing sellers of a taxed commodity is lower than the consumers' demand by the amount of the tax. Because of the shift in demand, the market equilibrium quantity under the tax is less than it is in the absence of the tax. The tax, then, distorts resource allocation: Under the tax, the marginal unit is valued at more than it costs; expanding production would produce a net gain. The tax, however, creates a wedge between the incentives of consumers and those of producers, thus preventing the realization of that gain.

Economists have argued that this tax analysis applies directly to the share contract. I shall use Figure 3.1, which I adapted from Cheung (1969, p. 43), to present this argument. In Figure 3.1 the value of the tenant's marginal product on a plot of a given size is M_{PL} and his or her market wage is W. Were the tenant self-employed, she or he would apply L^* units of time to the farm. The landlord, however, receives a share, r, of the output. The tenant whose share of the output is $(1 - r)$ retains only

34

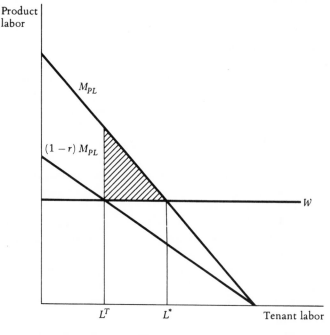

Figure 3.1

$(1 - r)$ of his own marginal product and will apply L^T units of time to the farm to maximize his wealth. For units of labor between L^T and L^*, the output value of the tenant exceeds the wage rate; however, the tenant will prefer to sell these units of labor service in the market because her share in the farm output is less than W per unit of labor. Such tenants, then, will stop short of producing the output when the value of their marginal product equals their alternative earning. The shaded area in Figure 3.1 is the alleged inefficiency induced by the share contract, which is likened to the tax distortion.

As Cheung demonstrates, this analysis is seriously flawed. Given the tenant's share of $1 - r$, L^T may appear as the tenants' optimal level of labor input. However, if the tenant is free to apply as much labor as he wishes, he can increase his income by becoming a share-tenant on two farms and spending half of L^T units of time in each. Indeed, the tenant will do best by working a tiny bit on each of several farms. Even on only one farm, the tenant earns on average more than W per unit of time. Consequently, $1 - r$ exceeds the tenant's equilibrium share. Tenants may compete simply by lowering the share they are willing to accept, but then the equilibrium labor input will fall as well. The logical conclusion of the process would entail share-tenants earning no rent, while their input would plummet to zero. This model, then, suffers from an internal inconsistency.

Before I turn to Cheung's solution, it should be noted that the tax analogy contains two implicit – and by no means innocent – assumptions. The first is that landlords find it prohibitively expensive to stipulate and police the amount of labor input. The second is that landlords encounter no cost in policing the receipt of their share of the output. Whereas either assumption may be a good approximation of real circumstances in any particular case, the two are unlikely to hold true simultaneously. Similarly, implicit in the traditional approach to the share contract are the assumptions that the cost of monitoring output is always zero and that the cost of monitoring labor input is always prohibitive: these assumptions are ad hoc. Models based on ad hoc assumptions are likely to be refuted when put to an empirical test.

In his ground-breaking work on the theory of share tenancy, which he tested empirically against observed practices in China, Cheung (1969) makes several points that are pertinent to the present discussion. First, he notes that sharecropping is unlikely to have been inefficient, given its long history of survival. Second, consistent with the Coase Theorem, in a world of zero transactions costs the share contract will yield an efficient outcome, as will other contract forms, because contractors can costlessly add and police contract stipulations in such a way that all inefficiency is eliminated. Third, in attempting to add empirical content to the Coase Theorem, Cheung spells out some of the stipulations that were necessary for efficiency to have been attained in sharecropping. He finds that practices in China were consistent with the implications he derives involving fixed plot size, required levels of other inputs, and restrictions on allowable crops. Since the implementation of these conditions consumes resources, the question remains as to why share tenancy was nevertheless utilized. Cheung argues that risk aversion may explain the prevalence of share tenancy because under share tenancy the landlord and the tenant share the vagaries of variations in output and in output value. Whereas Cheung's critique of the received analysis, which claims that the share contract distorts the allocation of resources, is well taken, his risk-aversion explanation is not.

Risk aversion does not satisfactorily explain the share contract. Attitude toward risk is a matter of taste. If, as we usually assume, taste is a personal matter that may vary unpredictably among individuals, an explanation based on risk aversion is not refutable. Moreover, how someone may act with regard to a risky prospect depends on his or her other actions and how risky they are – something we usually do not know. Under uniformity of taste toward risk, risk aversion is a function of such observable variables as wealth. Even then, the explanation of sharecropping is still insufficient. In a zero transaction cost world, share-cropping alone is not an attractive method of sharing risk. Share contracting does distribute the crop of a single plot between the two parties, but there are other ways to distribute variability that can remove more of the risk. For instance, because two persons residing on opposite sides of the globe are not subject to common random forces, pooling the risks between them reduces the risk each would face alone. Under the assumption of costless transactions, such pooling would involve no added costs and thus would be practiced. In reality, of course, transacting is costly, rendering some risk-pooling difficult to effect. When transacting is costly, however, all contract forms are costly. Sharing may be selected in that case not only for its effect on risk but also because of some properties of transaction costs. Moreover, when transacting is costly, other contracts may be chosen in spite of their riskiness. Later in this chapter I will offer a transaction cost hypothesis to explain sharing; in subsequent chapters I will provide transaction cost hypotheses to explain other forms of organization, assuming throughout that people are risk-neutral.[2]

THREE METHODS OF COLLABORATION BETWEEN OWNERS OF LAND AND OWNERS OF LABOR

Given the total amounts of land and labor, there is some plot size or, more generally, some size distribution of plots that maximizes total output. Only a fraction of workers, however, own the commensurate amount of land. Those who own more land than they alone can most profitably cultivate can gain by cooperating with those whose holdings are too small. In order to realize the gains, the factor owners must contract with each other. I will here consider three methods by which two owners can collaborate and in which ownership patterns are preserved: (1) the wage contract, (2) the rental contract, and (3) the share contract. A discussion of the consolidation of ownership will follow.

It was pointed out earlier that individual specimens of neither land nor labor are uniform. Before analyzing the general case in which both factors are variable, I will consider the special cases in which either the land or the labor *is* uniform. Suppose that land is entirely uniform and un-

---

[2] When the sole contractual problem between tenant and landlord is the method of dividing output, the role of risk aversion seems both simple and important. As a rule, however, many sources of variability confront the parties. The effect of crop-sharing on overall riskiness then becomes less clear and less important. For instance, it is not at all clear how transferring the maintenance of irrigation ditches from the landlord to the tenant affects the distribution of risk.

changeable. If collaboration is by a wage contract, workers can gain by shirking, exerting themselves less than they would were they self-employed. Output is subject to variability because of random factors affecting output directly *and* because workers' contributions to output vary. It is, therefore, difficult to differentiate the effect of change in effort from random factors. Under the given conditions, the wage contract requires supervision. Since supervision is costly, economy in its use will be exercised. Workers are expected to take advantage of the opportunity to shirk. They will not work as hard as would self-employed workers. As attractive as the opportunity to shirk may seem to a wage worker, he or she is bound to lose as a result of it. Wage payment will be adjusted to the expected reduction in effort; workers are paid, on average, for what work they accomplish. Such workers would prefer to work harder and be paid more because they operate at a point at which the cost to them of an extra unit of effort is less than the corresponding value of the increase in output brought about by that effort; however, the cost of effecting such an arrangement exceeds the gain it would generate. The allocation of resources under the wage contract is not optimal here.

Tenants who operate under share contracts retain a portion – but not all – of their marginal product. Although the incentive to shirk is not as strong here as it is in the wage contract, it is induced by the same factors, and the preceding discussion of the wage contract applies.

Tenants who collaborate with landowners by renting their land pay a fixed amount for its use. Actual output will differ from expected output because of random fluctuations and to the extent that the tenants alter their own efforts. Because land is uniform, it does not contribute to output variability; the tenants' expected output varies only as a function of their own effort. The tenant is the "residual claimant": Barring bankruptcy, the landlord receives a fixed amount, while the tenant receives whatever is left over after paying the rent (of course, this difference may be a negative amount). Apart from the random element, the tenants' rewards are strictly a function of their own efforts. In the case of uniform land, tenants will make the optimal effort under the fixed rent contract.

The analysis of the situation where land is heterogeneous and labor (and labor effort) is uniform is the mirror image of the one just presented. When labor is uniform, wage contracts make expected output solely a function of the quality of the land. Landlords have the appropriate incentive to maintain and improve their land and will not gain from misrepresenting its quality. In this case the landlords are the residual claimants and are the only ones affected by their own actions. A rental (or a share) contract would be inefficient here, producing less total income for the contracting parties.[3] The more efficient contract, that of the fixed wage, would prevail under such conditions.

In reality, neither land nor labor is uniform. It follows that all three contract forms are subject to efficiency problems. When discrepancies between costs and valuations are inevitable, an arrangement in which such discrepancies are observed cannot be thought of as inefficient. Inefficiency implies preventable waste – waste that would not occur if people were to maximize. In an imperfect world, even the best solution is still subject to discrepancies between marginal costs and marginal valuations; not all such discrepancies can be eliminated economically. When we discover discrepancies, our task is to determine how resource allocation will change when the costs of or the returns from reducing the discrepancies change. In order to be able to analyze changes in resource allocation, a more detailed analysis of the nature of variability is necessary.

THE EFFECTS OF VARIABILITY WITHIN FACTORS

Because it is commonly, though only implicitly, assumed that land is uniform and unchangeable, it is instructive to examine the nature of land and the effects of variability in it. Each acre of land differs from all others – even from the ones adjacent to it – in a variety of ways: incidence of rocks; steepness; degree of soil erosion; presence of various nutrients; level of moisture; and exposure to wind and sun. Land parcels also differ in terms of access to groundwater, quality and quantity of irrigation canals, availability of pumping equipment, types of roads serving them, and distance to markets. Moreover, the ease of exploiting such features also varies.

Land use would be efficient if landlords were compensated by users of land for the exact reduction in land value. Because land is not uniform, however, the exact evaluation of these effects requires measurement at every spot. The fact that exact and comprehensive measurements are prohibitively costly leads to measurements that are neither exact nor comprehensive. Indeed, certain features may not be measured at all. Contracts explicitly delineate some specific attributes of the transaction. They also implicitly delineate others that are governed by common law. They

---

[3] The fact that the fixed-rent contract has not been claimed to be inefficient suggests that land (inclusive of the improvement and equipment that accompanied it) has been viewed as unchangeable. On the other hand, economists have been quick to criticize Henry George's single-tax proposal, pointing out that since his assumption that land was unchangeable was too unrealistic, his policy conclusions were rendered useless. Had economists been consistent in recognizing in all their applications that land is changeable, it is less likely that the share contract would have been singled out as the only inefficient tenure contract. Either the fixed-rent contract would also have been considered inefficient or both contracts would have been recognized as efficient.

do not delineate all of them. Because attributes that are prohibitively costly to specify are part of the transaction and will be exploited, the contracts between the owners of productive services will not award each his or her precise contribution.[4] Among the unspecified attributes, some are subject to control by the buyer and some by the seller. By "control" I mean one's freedom to manipulate the particular unspecified attribute without making marginal payments to others.

Contracting is viewed here as a strictly symmetrical operation. The parties contract with each other because both own productive services that stand to increase in total value as a result of the cooperation between them: *Each* can contribute to the collaboration. I assume that contract terms are determined by competition and, therefore, that those contracts that maximize the value of each transaction net of all the associated costs will prevail. Thus, in spite of the marginal inequalities – the violation of the Pareto conditions – no true inefficiencies can be present.

THE FIXED-RENT CONTRACT

In this section, I will analyze the nature of the deadweight losses that arise with a fixed-rent contract as a result of not pricing attributes at the margin, and in the following section I will indicate methods available to contain these deadweight losses. Suppose a tenant rents a plot of land on a fixed-rent basis. I assume that soil nutrients are placed under the tenant's control, permitting the extraction of whatever amount he or she wishes without paying a marginal charge, and that the maintenance of land improvements is left under the landowner's control and not priced on the margin either. The three parts of Figure 3.2, depicting different aspects of the land rental, will be used to analyze the nature of the equilibrium and the forces that lead to it; parts A and B reflect behavior within the transaction, and part C relates to market behavior.

The horizontal axis in part A is the per-acre amount of nutrients extracted from the soil and the vertical axis is dollars per acre. L_N is the marginal fall in land value due to the depletion of the nutrients. Although to the tenant the nutrient is free, its use is constrained by the cost of extraction. C_N is the marginal cost of extracting the nutrients – arising, for instance, from the need to use water to transform the nutrient into a form that plants can utilize. $C_N + L_N$ is the sum of the two costs. D_N is the demand for the nutrients reflecting the (marginal) increase in the

---

[4]Holmstrom and Milgrom (1991) have also studied complex (multitask) relationships. Using the principal-agent model, they focus on the (risk-averse) agent performance of the interrelated tasks. They do not consider the potential for moral hazard by the "principal," as I do. Eswaran and Kotwal (1985) present a double moral hazard model.

Contract choice

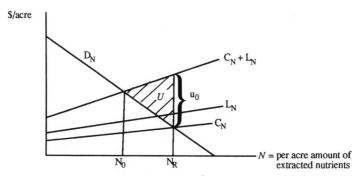

A: per-acre cost of and demand for (valuation of) nutrient

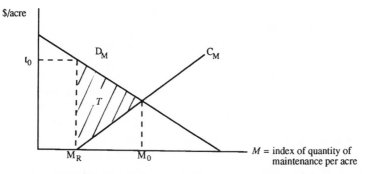

B: per-acre cost of and demand for (valuation of) maintenance

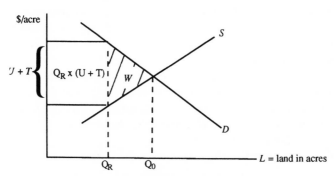

C: market for land under fixed rent contracts

Figure 3.2

value of output as the amount of extracted nutrients increases. A self-employed landowner will extract N_0, the quantity at which D_N and $C_N + L_N$ intersect. Since the land rent contract does not charge for nutrient use, the tenant does not pay, on the margin, for the depletion of the nutrient. He or she will extract N_R, the quantity at which D_N intersects C_N, the latter being the cost borne by the tenant.[5] It is as if the tenant receives an implicit per-acre subsidy at the rate of u_0 that is equal to the height of L_N, the marginal fall in land value, at N_R. Since the tenant will deplete the nutrient at the rate of N_R, whereas the self-employed worker will deplete it at the rate of N_0, the per-acre loss due to the excessive use of the nutrient by a renter is the shaded area U.

Although the tenant controls the use of the nutrient and is able to extract an "excessive" amount, such as N_R, per acre, that control is ultimately at his own expense. A tenant who could somehow commit to use only N_0 soil nutrients per acre would produce a lower output. However, he would have to pay a lower fixed rent such that his net income could increase by an amount up to the area U. As was pointed out earlier, this is a general phenomenon. On average, those able to shirk, to cheat, or to enjoy "free" perks must, under competition, pay for the privilege by an amount that *exceeds* in expected terms the value of the privilege. The privilege is granted only because it is too costly to eliminate.

Part B of Figure 3.2 shows the per-acre level of maintenance and improvements, assumed to be under the landowner's control. The horizontal axis is (an index of) the per-acre level of maintenance. C_M is that part of the cost of the landowner's maintenance activity that affects the contract-period crop, and D_M is the demand for maintenance within the contract period. Assuming that there are no cross effects between maintenance and nutrients, a self-employed landowner will operate at the intersection of D_M and C_M, providing maintenance at a rate of M_0. When the land is rented out and maintenance is not stipulated in the contract, the landlord, who does not gain from the contribution of maintenance to current output, will supply the amount of M_R.[6] It is as if the landlord pays a 100 percent tax on the improvement's contribution, which here amounts to t_0 per acre. The per-acre loss from maintenance at level M_R rather than M_0 is the shaded area T.

Part C shows the market for land under fixed-rent contracts. Were

[5] Given measurement costs, the tenant will use such nutrients to the point at which the estimated rather than the actual net gain from an extra unit is zero. For simplicity of exposition, such inaccuracies are ignored whenever the consequences are not germane to the argument.
[6] M_R can be greater than zero because current maintenance, which enhances the post-contract value of improvements, may also benefit current production. A landlord will lubricate his water pump during the current period if it is the most economical way to enhance his income during future periods.

marginal discrepancies absent, D and S would be the relevant demand and supply curves, and Q_0 would be the equilibrium quantity. As contracts for rented land fail to price some attributes, account must be taken of the resulting discrepancies, which are part of the costs of transacting. To simplify the exposition, I assume that the discrepancies occur only in nutrients and maintenance. The quantity $U + T$ is the combined per-acre loss to renters and landlords; it arises from their failure to stipulate and police the use of nutrients and the level of maintenance. Assuming that the average and the marginal losses due to the discrepancies are equal, Q_R, the quantity for which the height of the demand curve exceeds that of the supply curve by $U + T$, is the equilibrium amount of rented land. $U + T$ is the loss on the marginal acre. The total loss on the land being rented is $(U + T)Q_R$. In addition, there is a loss due to too little land rental, shown as the shaded triangular area W in panel C.[7, 8]

METHODS FOR RESTRAINING LOSSES

Labor and land are complex factors, each possessing many attributes, but contracts between pairs of owners are usually quite simple. How, then, are the individual attributes controlled by contract, and what forces determine which contract will maximize the value of the resources? A fixed-rent land contract can simply stipulate duration and rent; alternatively, it can be as detailed as the contracting parties wish it to be.[9] Whereas contractors are free to stipulate whatever they wish, not all attributes are worth stipulating and monitoring. Any attribute that is not stipulated and that can be varied becomes a free attribute. Tenants who are in control of such an attribute will use extra units so long as they generate added positive (net) income; landlords will similarly use attributes under their control.

Although by assumption the loss associated with free attributes is too costly to avert directly, it can be controlled in two distinct ways. First, contract stipulations regarding attributes related to the ones subject to excessive exploitation or inadequate provision may be altered. Second, an altogether different contract may be used, one that controls those attributes left uncontrolled under the first contract.

[7] In this case, the quantity $W + (U + T)Q_R$ is the cost of transaction as I define it in Barzel 1985. See also Allen 1991.

[8] Panel C incorporates only two unspecified attributes, one controlled by the tenant and one by the landlord. Generalizing for any number of independent attributes, however, is straightforward.

[9] In either case, a mechanism to enforce contract performance is required. Such a mechanism is usually provided partly by the contractors and partly by the courts. The existence of such a mechanism will here be taken as a given.

Manipulating related attributes

In the conventional land-rent model it is implicitly assumed that land is unchangeable. This implies that the supply elasticities of all its unspecified attributes are zero; under these conditions the fixed rent contract is efficient (given risk-neutrality, which I assume). However, land can be altered. Cheung (1969) points out that when the cost of transacting is zero, efficiency can always be attained because the transactors can then costlessly fix the level of any factor they supply. By fixing all attributes at the desired levels, the over- or under-utilization of any attribute will be avoided. I will here elaborate on the theme of operating on the levels of land attributes but will drop the costless transacting assumption.

Transactors can gain by constraining their actions so that they reduce utilization where it would otherwise be excessive and increase provision where it would otherwise be inadequate. I here concentrate on reducing the use of soil nutrients, an attribute that is free to the tenant. Consider an attribute that is complementary to the soil nutrient but was not initially made part of the exchange contract. Suppose that a self-employed individual would have used the complementary attribute at a per-acre rate of W_0, and that the landowner can, at a low cost, fix the level of the complementary attribute. Fixing the level of the complementary attribute at W_0 will render the cost of using the free attribute around the equilibrium point less elastic,[10] thereby lowering the associated distortion. For example, suppose that water-use is the attribute complementary to the extraction of a soil nutrient. The landlord can reduce the tenant's cost elasticity for the extraction of the soil nutrient and the associated distortion by supplying up to W_0 water per acre.

The effect of fixing the amount of water at W_0 is shown in Figure 3.3, which elaborates on part A of Figure 3.2. Each point on C_N is arrived at by using the combination of inputs that minimizes the cost of extracting the corresponding amount of the nutrient. The amount of water used in the process of cost minimization of extracting the amount N_0 is W_0. When W is fixed at up to W_0, the cost of extracting the nutrient shifts from C_N – which is derived under the assumption that the tenant can adjust the amount of water purchased – to $C_N|W_0$, where W is fixed at W_0. The latter is less elastic at N_0 and to the right of it. To the left of N_0, however, the constraint is not binding, and in that region $C_N|W_0$ coincides with C_N. When W is fixed at W_0, the use of nutrients falls from N_R

---

[10]The general proposition regarding the demand (supply) curve is that around an equilibrium position, fixing the level of either a complementary or a substitute good, the own demand (supply) elasticity will be less than it is when the quantity of the related good is allowed to adjust (see Silberberg 1990).

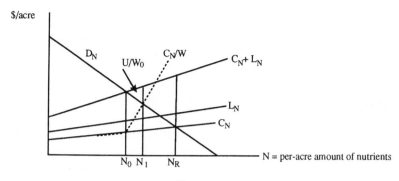

Figure 3.3

to N_1. The total loss is reduced from U (Figure 3.2, part A) to $U|W_0$ (a triangle in Figure 3.3).

Although W_0 is the amount of water used by a self-employed individual, constraining W to W_0 does not quite minimize the distortion. It will be minimized when the amount of water is restricted to an amount (somewhat) less than W_0. As the amount used falls below W_0, a new distortion is introduced in the sense that water use becomes "too small." But as the quantity of soil nutrient extracted falls with the reduction in the amount of water, the associated loss also falls initially at a rate faster than the increase in the new one induced by the insufficient use of water (the "envelope" theorem). Some value of $W - W_1$, such that $W_1 < W_0 -$ is the optimal level of water needed.

The landlord may operate on additional inputs. He may impose alternative or additional restrictions, such as stipulating that the tenant must supply minimal amounts of factors that are substitutes for the (free) nutrient, thereby further lowering the demand elasticity (and the demand) for the nutrient. A similar argument applies to attributes controlled by the landlord. Consider a factor complementary to maintenance. If the tenant agrees to supply an amount of that complementary factor equal to (or, preferably, somewhat greater than) the amount a self-employed tenant would have provided, the landlord's supply of maintenance will increase toward its optimal amount, thus reducing the loss associated with that factor. For example, the landlord will provide more pumping equipment if the tenant agrees to lubricate it.

Free attribute losses can be also reduced by manipulating the prices of commodities related to the free attributes. For instance, if the price of a commodity that is a substitute for a free attribute is reduced, the demand for the free attribute will decline, as will the associated loss. A landlord who wishes to reduce the tenant's use of an unpriced soil nutrient and

45

finds it too costly to police the use of a complementary fertilizer may subsidize the tenant's purchase of the fertilizer. In order to further reduce transaction costs, some commodities that are substitutes for unpriced attributes may be supplied at no marginal charge in order to reduce the use of these attributes.[11]

Duration is another contract feature that affects the parties' behavior with regard to attributes. A wheatland owner may find a one-year rental contract to be satisfactory. On the other hand, in the case of an orchard, the care and maintenance of the trees, which can be most efficiently provided by the tenant, become free attributes to a one-year tenant, whereas a longer-term rental contract enhances the tenant's incentive for care and maintenance, thus reducing the tenant's exploitation of these attributes.

Consider a tenancy contract of one year's duration.[12] Work animals or tractors supplied by the landlord are most likely to be severely depreciated by year end if the tenant is in charge of their upkeep. The tenant's demand elasticity for the services that result in wear and tear is high, and the associated loss is large. If, however, the tenant has to supply such items, no shirking in maintenance is expected. Generally, the tenant here gains much more from affecting the value of the capital more than the landlord does. Because he or she, rather than the landowner, owns this input, the tenant bears the bulk of the reduction in value its use induces. He or she will then use this capital carefully, which is likely to more than compensate for the greater difficulty of raising capital.

A similar argument applies to land improvements. These may seem to be an integral part of the land and thus a "responsibility" of the landlord. The less long lasting their effects, however, the less inclined the landlord will be to perform these functions while the contract is in force. The problem becomes less acute if shorter-term improvements such as fertilizing and weed control are assigned to or simply assumed by the tenant. It is expected that the contract will assign the shorter-term improvements to the tenant and the longer-term ones to the landlord; the longer the duration of the contract, the further the dividing line is expected to move toward the longer-term improvements.[13] Since the effects of the improve-

---

[11] The success of a price subsidy *depends* on the presence of a particular transaction cost – that of reselling the subsidized commodity. That cost must be high enough so that there is no gain from reselling the commodity.

[12] Recall the assumption that the relationship between tenant and landlord is governed only by the contract; the expectation of renewal is ignored.

[13] A landlord may undertake an improvement before signing the contract even if it is optimal to undertake it in the middle of the contract period, since he is not expected to undertake it after the contract is signed. The rent he can charge, however, depends in part on the improvements he provides. Allen and Lueck (1992) present evidence on this point.

ments are seldom confined to a particular period, each may be required to provide a minimal amount.

The duration of the contract, which is endogenously determined, often plays a major part in better aligning the parties' incentives. The duration of the contract is understood to be the length of the period in which the parties cede control of some attributes to each other. Changes in the duration of the contract affect the parties' incentives to exploit free attributes. This can easily be seen by comparing a tenancy contract that covers the planting but not the harvesting season with a contract that covers both. Given the shorter contract duration, the tenant is not expected to do any planting, since planting is a "land improvement": the landlord will receive the entire output and the tenant will pay a 100 percent tax. The tenant's incentive for planting is restored by extending the contract period to cover the harvest season. The longer the span between planting and harvesting, the longer the expected duration of tenure.[14]

The task of caring for the trees need not be assigned to the tenant, just as equipment maintenance is not necessarily a tenant's task. Such assignments are a matter of choice: The contractors are expected to assign the provision of particular attributes to whichever party is more suitable. The existence of such a choice points to another aspect of the loss-restraining problem. It may seem that in the land-rent contract it is clear which inputs each contractor furnishes: The landowner supplies the land and the tenant the labor. The recognition, however, that any commodity is a collection of attributes suggests that the real situation is more complex. Improvements, for instance, are obviously not an integral part of the land, and the contractors are free to decide which party will take charge of any of them.[15] More generally, the contractors are free to decide which party should furnish particular attributes.

With regard to each attribute, one might ask: Which of the two parties will be more inclined to affect the (net) value of output by manipulating that attribute? The principle I applied earlier to labor and land applies to individual attributes as well. If the party that will be more inclined to affect the outcome by varying the level of an attribute is put in control of

---

[14] The incentive to exploit free attributes intensifies toward the end of the contract period. The more acute this problem, the more likely it is that the parties will sign a new contract before the older one expires. In professional sports, such phasing in of contracts is common both for athletes and for coaches. The motivation is to prevent underperformance by athletes as the expiration of their own contracts approaches, while avoiding the overuse of athletes by coaches whose contracts are about to expire.

[15] If landlords are legally required to keep certain improvements present on the plot at the time the contract is signed, there is no need to spell this out in the contract. Similarly, if a landlord plans to maintain the improvements, she or he will not require such maintenance from the tenant. Some contracts may appear to be lacking in detail but may, nevertheless, differ significantly from similarly worded tenancy contracts in areas in which the particular improvements are simply absent.

that attribute, thereby becoming the residual claimant of its variability, losses will be minimized. If, for example, land is rented out on an annual basis, the maintenance of long-lasting improvements will tend to be placed in the landlord's charge, since landlords are the chief beneficiaries of proper maintenance because of the higher rents they will be able to charge in future periods.

Changing the contract form

In the preceding section it was shown that the fixed-rent contract places various land attributes in the public domain and that the associated losses can be lowered by manipulating the prices and quantities of related goods. The overuse of those contract attributes that are not directly controlled may be curbed but cannot be eliminated. It is proper to ask whether collaboration between owners of land and owners of labor should occur through a contract that is an alternative to the land-rent contract.

Changing the assignment of responsibilities can be radically different from changing the stipulations of an existing contract. It can instead be effected by altering the unit by which the transaction is conducted. Such a change in units affects the whole structure of attribute ownership, or responsibility, and the associated incentive system. The contract between the owner of land and the owner of labor can use acres as the basic transaction unit – the rental contract – or it can use man-hours as the basic unit – the employment contract. Shifting from one contract to the other constitutes a global change in the tax-subsidy structure; it completely alters the supply and demand of the various unpriced attributes. For instance, since an employed worker's pay is not, on the margin, a function of output value, he or she does not gain from exploiting the soil nutrients. This change will, in turn, affect the nature of the output – indeed, the choice of what to produce. A switch from one contract form to another may even alter the desired characteristics of exchange partners, in effect changing their identity. The basic character of the problem, however, remains unchanged. Each party will overuse those attributes that are both controlled by her or him and subsidized by the other party, and each will reduce the supply of those attributes which he or she subsidizes. The wage contract, for instance, seldom stipulates all workplace amenities, and the employer is expected to shirk in providing them.

The decision of whether to adopt a land-rent or a wage contract depends on which of the two results in a smaller total loss from the marginal discrepancies, thus maximizing the net gain of the cooperation. Leaving aside, for the moment, the discussion of sharing, it is clear that the two contracts cannot be compared marginally. The one that will maximize the net value of the resources is expected to be adopted. Conditions can be specified, however, under which a shift from one contract form to the other is expected to occur. For example, the more valuable the land attributes that are difficult to measure and to police, the more likely it is that the wage contract will be adopted.

Any contract is subject to problems of non-optimal use; therefore, no single contract is best under all circumstances. Changes in the circumstances that affect contract choice may be gradual, but the change in contract *form* cannot be; either it takes place or it does not. Thus, a comparison between contract forms must be "global": total net values must be calculated in order to determine which contract generates the highest net gain. Economists are not equipped to make such comparisons directly. Conditions can be spelled out, however, under which a switch from one form to another is likely. Turning to the three contract forms, one refutable implication of the immediately preceding model is that when market wage rises relative to land rent, the contract form will shift away from the wage contract, which induces a (relatively) careless use of labor, to the land-rent contract (though perhaps first to the share contract), which induces a relatively careless use of land. As a prelude to comparing the different contract forms, we should first examine the practice of share contracting.

ADVANTAGES AND DISADVANTAGES OF SHARING

The share tenancy contract stands halfway between the fixed-rent and the wage contract. When sharing, both landowner and tenant are residual claimants because each is remunerated by a fraction of whatever the output is. At the same time, each gains from shirking: The landowner will not maintain land improvements as vigorously as he or she would have under the wage contract, and the tenant will not work as hard as he or she would have under the fixed-rent contract. The margins subject to distortion under the share contract include all those of the other two contracts. In addition, the specification and monitoring of output are likely to consume more resources under the share contract than under the other contract forms. Although more margins are subject to distortion when the contract calls for sharing, the loss from some margins of distortion is reduced more than proportionately. Adopting a new perspective on the previously discussed tax analogy may demonstrate how the share contract can result in a lower level of distortions than that associated with the other two contracts.

The analysis of tax distortions is standard fare in taxation literature. It is well known that the distortion associated with a tax (or with a subsidy) rises as the square of the tax (or subsidy) rate. Thus, the welfare-loss triangle of a 10 percent tax on a commodity is (approximately) four times as large as that of a 5 percent tax on the same commodity. In the wage contract, to the extent that supervision is not perfect, the reduction in effort is a free attribute available to the worker, because the worker is not penalized for the reduced effort. It is as if the worker were to pay a 100 percent tax on the increase in output induced by greater effort. Similarly, under the fixed-rent contract it is as if the tenant were to receive a 100 percent subsidy on soil nutrients and the landlord were to pay a 100 percent tax on land improvements, yielding returns within the contract period. In a share contract the taxes are reduced from 100 percent to the worker's share in the case of the extra effort and to the landlord's share in the case of the maintenance expenses. Since the deadweight loss rises quadratically with the tax rate, the rate reduction brought about by sharing results in a more than proportionate reduction in losses. For instance, a fifty-fifty sharing arrangement would reduce the distortions from each of the taxed attributes to one-fourth of their levels at the 100 percent tax or subsidy. The proposition, however, does not apply to the subsidized attributes, since these continue to receive a 100 percent subsidy. For example, to the tenant the nutrient is fully subsidized under both the fixed-rent and the share contract. Whereas *all* of these items are taxed or subsidized in a share contract, compared with only about *half* of them being taxed or subsidized when one or the other of the two contract forms is used, the quadratic relationship is capable of lessening the total burden under the share contract to a level below that of the burden either of the other forms generates. The share contract, however, entails an increase in monitoring costs, which may tip the scales against it.

Monitoring serves to reduce the losses associated with margins of distortion. The monitoring of each margin of distortion, however, entails its own start-up cost. Since the share contract is subject to more margins of distortion than are the other two contracts, its costs of monitoring are higher. The gains the share contract is capable of generating in reduced distortions may not be large enough, and the share contract may fail to be adopted. As conditions gradually shift, favoring, say, the wage contract over the fixed-rent contract, the share contract becomes attractive as an intermediate step; nevertheless, because of the required extra monitoring costs, the share contract may be skipped altogether.[16] As the fixed-rent contract becomes less attractive, the fraction of rent contracts is expected to fall and the fraction of wage contracts is expected to increase;

[16] As the value of the contributions of the two parties becomes more equal, a sharing arrangement is more likely to emerge. This is because a fifty-fifty sharing formula tends to yield the highest reduction in distortions and is also simpler to administer than others.

but it is not possible to state, a priori, whether the fraction of share contracts will increase or fall.

I have thus far focused on the costs and gains associated with fixed wages, fixed rents, and share contracts between owners of land and labor. Although different contracts encounter different incentive problems, every exchange, and therefore every contract, is subject to some such problem. The sole-ownership arrangement is free of those contracting problems that arise when land and labor are not owned by the same person. It might appear that sole ownership should be the preferred method of operation. However, the sole-ownership arrangement is subject to two sets of transaction costs associated with owning all of the inputs in a production process. The first set of costs arises because the pattern of ownership of productive non-human assets is extremely unlikely to match fully the ownership pattern of human skills that would have generated the highest output. Total output, then, can be increased if people exchange productive assets in order to arrive at a better match of resources. To accomplish this, owners of labor would have to borrow in order to buy the land with which to work. For this to occur, transacting must be reintroduced – here the transaction between borrower and lender replacing that between owner of labor and owner of land – and it cannot be determined a priori that the transaction between the former two would yield a higher net gain than the transaction between the latter two.

The second, equally important set of costs of sole ownership exists due to the losses in specialization that occur when one individual owns and uses all of the productive inputs.[17] Although sole ownership does remove the incentive to shirk, the gains from specialization are also forgone. In order to maximize the return from their land, landowners will engage in such activities as maintenance work and prevention of erosion. The owners of labor will invest in such activities as maintaining and improving their cultivation skills. One person who owns both assets cannot profitably specialize as much as two individual owners of two assets. However, to the extent that collaboration will take place, the owners of the collaborating factors will also acquire skills in protecting their assets against capture by their partners. For instance, the landowner will acquire information about methods of reducing the overuse of nutrients. The notion that land and labor are sufficient to produce output is a gross oversimplification: Many production factors determine the output. Farmers are sel-

---

[17] See Eswaran and Kotwal 1985.

dom if ever the sole owners of all inputs. A present-day sole-owner farmer in the United States would, among other things, have to own and operate a spray plane and conduct plant research and development. As markets grow larger, the potential gains from specialization should increase; any one person should benefit from relinquishing the ownership of various assets (or attributes of some asset) and engaging in contracting with owners of other inputs in order to acquire the corresponding services. The gains deriving from sole ownership must be balanced against the falling output caused by the commensurate lower level of specialization.

SOME IMPLICATIONS

The contracting model discussed thus far can generate many implications with regard to actual tenancy practices. Because information problems are at the heart of the high cost of transacting, I will concentrate on those implications that are a direct consequence of these problems. Two sources of change in information costs will be considered, one associated with the introduction of a new crop and the other with the arrival of new workers.

When a crop new to an area becomes profitable, information on how well it will do in different locations within the area is more costly to obtain than is similar information on old crops. Landowners who personally cultivate only part of their holdings and contract with others to cultivate the rest of their land know, as a rule, more about their land than do their tenants. Because they are also the main beneficiaries of good decisions about new crops, the discrepancy in landlord-versus-tenant knowledge for the new crop is likely to be higher than it was for the old crop. Tenants who are offered fixed-rent contracts may suspect that the rent landlords' demand is excessive and that the landlords are exaggerating the productiveness of their plots in growing the new crop. Such suspicions are hard to allay; hence tenants' demand for land and their associated counteroffers are likely to be low. Wage contracts are free of this particular problem because landlords who pay fixed wages bear the entire new-crop risk, about which they are better informed than are tenants. Landowners who switch to the new crop are more likely to offer wage contracts to their tenants than they were with the old, established crop. In addition, it is expected that with the passage of time the direction of the trend will be reversed: The cost of determining the suitability of land parcels for the new crop will decline, inducing the readoption of fixed-rent contracts where they were preferred before.

Another information problem arises concerning immigration. Little is known about how workers who are new to an area will perform. Land-owners are reluctant to commit themselves to paying new workers the prevailing wage. Given the lack of knowledge regarding workers' abilities and attitudes, the demand for the services of such workers and, consequently, the wages offered are likely to be low. A new worker who believes that he or she is more productive than the wage being offered indicates can "guarantee" his or her output by offering to operate as a fixed-rent tenant. These workers, then, bear the onus of the information problem. It is expected that relatively more new workers than established ones will operate as fixed-rent tenants. Moreover, new tenants will be given parcels that are more difficult to exploit, such as those containing few improvements. Some old-time tenants may acquire a reputation for being gentle on the land and on improvements; these individuals will be the favored fixed-rent tenants on the easy-to-exploit parcels. Newcomers do not have such reputations and are therefore expected to get land parcels for which the lack of information makes less difference. Here, too, the trend is expected to be reversed as the new workers become more established in the area.

CONCLUSION

The owners of labor and of land can increase the value of their assets by collaborating, because total output is rendered larger than it would be were they to operate alone. However, effecting the collaboration, is itself costly because it is difficult to prevent wealth capture when cooperation is attempted. Measuring each factor's contribution to output is necessary for cooperation to be successful. Such measurements are costly and therefore will not be precise. This lack of precision, coupled with the variability in output due to unpredictable factors such as the weather, implies that individuals can gain at each other's expense and that they will spend resources in order to capture these gains. Together owners of labor and owners of land (bolstered by competition from other owners) will adopt the contract form that generates the largest net output value where maximization is subject to conventional production costs as well as to the costs associated with the capture of wealth.

Neither labor nor land is uniform; specimens of each vary in terms of the levels of their respective attributes. The contract between the owners will therefore attempt to control not only the factors as a whole but also various individual attributes. Some of these attributes may be controlled directly (e.g., a tenant pays for irrigation water supplied by the landlord); those difficult to control directly may be controlled indirectly by fixing quantities and altering prices. A basic principle underlying the maximiza-

Economic analysis of property rights

Source of losses from various contractual forms

	Policing labor	Policing land	Policing output	Lack of specializing
High losses	FW	FR	SC	SO
Intermediate losses	SC	SC	FW	SC
Low or no losses	FR, SO	FW,SO	SO,FR	FW, FR

SO: Sole owner of land and labor
SC: Share contract
FW: Fixed-wage contract
FR: Fixed-rent contract

tion process is that individual attributes will be placed under the control of the party that can more readily affect the net value of the outcome by manipulating the attribute.

The accompanying table catalogues and compares the losses associated with the various contractual arrangements analyzed in this chapter. This table clearly reveals that no single solution is best under all circumstances. As a situation changes, the form of organization will tend to change as well.

4

Divided ownership

In Chapter 3, I pointed out that in order to cooperate, resource owners must cede to each other control over some of the attributes of their resources. Since it is too costly to price every attribute, their use will be sub-optimal, and some potential gains will be forsaken as a result. Sole ownership of all of the resources involved would eliminate the deadweight loss associated with cooperation. However, sole ownership may result in yet a greater loss due to reduced specialization; if this is the case, it will not be chosen. It might appear that in the case of commodities or assets that consist of single physical entities rather than those that are more complex, sole ownership would be routinely adopted. But because most, if not all, transacted commodities have many attributes, multiple ownership of commodities may be preferred to sole ownership. In this chapter, I shall suggest sources of potential gains from multiple ownership, offer hypotheses regarding the form the division of ownership will take, and discuss the organizations that are expected to emerge to handle relations among the owners.

The physical entities I consider to be commodities or assets typically consist of many attributes, and often different subsets of asset-attributes are owned by different individuals. For instance, the economic and legal ownership of every asset subject to guarantee (or to liability) is divided between its holder and its guarantor; similarly, the ownership of every rented asset is divided between the nominal owner and the renter. Explaining the pattern of such ownership is central to the study of organization. My thesis is, first, that different individuals have comparative advantages in owning different attributes, and that individuals will assume ownership of the attributes accordingly. Second, as transactors' gain from affecting the outcome of an aspect of a transaction increases, they will assume more responsibility for the associated variability. That is, they will tend to assume a greater share of, and thus increasingly become residual claimants to, the income of the attributes they can affect more than they did before. The management of entities with divided ownership requires organization, which is one of the subjects of the present chapter. The discussion of divided ownership and its management is also a useful introduction to the firm, which is the subject of Chapter 5.

THE OWNERSHIP OF EQUIPMENT

Scale economies to equipment used in production are often asserted to be a major determinant of the size of the firm. (I shall elaborate on the firm and its size in Chapter 5.) In the standard model the size of the (competitive) firm is such that it fully exploits scale economies. In the following discussion I will concentrate on the ownership pattern for equipment, some of which is large-scale.

The exploitation of large-scale equipment requires input from many individuals. Since these individuals may attempt to gain at each other's expense, their interactions result in transaction costs. Maximization requires taking such costs into account and reducing their impact. It is convenient to introduce transaction costs here by considering problems associated with such a large scale. In the process of analyzing the effects of these costs, I shall show that the existence of scale economies associated with equipment is neither necessary nor sufficient for the existence of a large-scale organization. Although large-scale operations may also be associated with activities such as innovation and the research required for marketing and for the pricing of commodities, I here consider only the equipment's scale.

The potential for large-scale economies can be realized by a centralizing organization; alternatively, such economies may be realized by turning each resource owner into a residual claimant of his or her own operations, allowing each free, though not exclusive, access to the equipment. In the latter case, the individuals operating the large-scale equipment need not all belong to the same organization; each may assume full control of his or her niche of the operation.[1] They may accomplish this by raising capital, purchasing other inputs, and selling output. Presumably, if a large-scale organization is chosen, the participating owners of resources have opportunities to shirk. If each participant instead remains independent, each would have unrestricted access to "his" or "her" part of the equipment as well, rendering it common property, since various attributes of the large-scale activity are then left in the public domain.

I shall argue that, as a rule, the maximizing solution to the problem of the use of large-scale equipment is a mixture of the two forms of organi-

---

[1] In a classic study Allen (1966 [1929]) describes how in Birmingham in the 1860s workers operating independently of each other shared space and power sources in large factories.

zation. Of the resource owners associated with the operation, several subsets are expected to become residual claimants to different components of the large-scale operation. Within subsets containing more than one individual, however, individuals will operate as members of centralizing organizations.

I shall use three capital goods – a taxicab, a large machine, and an office building – to illustrate the nature of this problem.[2] Problems associated with the use of the first two goods will be described briefly, while the third will be explored more extensively. The following examples encompass most of the problems that arise when equipment is used, as well as the different methods for resolving them.

Although taxicabs are not large, a cab may be operated by two or three full-time operators. Consider, for example, the case in which a cab is operated by two individuals who share its ownership and drive it in shifts. The two may seem to operate as full-fledged partners. I suggest, however, that they will exploit the opportunities available to them to reduce common-property problems by making certain attributes exclusive properties.

Since the two drivers share ownership of the cab, its unpriced attributes will be consumed as if they were half free, thereby causing the cab to become, in part, common property.[3] This case corresponds to sharing in agriculture, except that here they share its use, since each of the two partners drives the car. The sharing, however, need not apply to all the attributes of the cab. For instance, the time slots allotted to each owner may be clearly delineated between the two; each then becomes the exclusive user of the cab for the appropriate sub-periods. Whether or not the use of gasoline will become common property depends on the accuracy of the fuel gauge. Assuming it is reasonably accurate, each may assume responsibility for the cost of his or her own fuel. The division of responsibility for the use of the tires depends on how easy it is to keep track of individuals' mileage (very easy) and tire damage, which depends on the type of road traveled and driving style (impractical). Thus, tire use is more likely to become common property than are time slots, perhaps also more likely than is the use of gasoline. Upholstery wear and tear is too costly to monitor and is likely to become common property. Consider, finally, why the engine may become common property. Suppose that engines designed for premium gasoline can also run on regular gasoline but are damaged by its use and, for the sake of illustration, that

---

[2] Divided ownership is not restricted to equipment. Until quite recently, many financial assets appeared to be "whole." In recent years, however, it has been found that they can be unbundled to reveal a rights structure of some complexity.

[3] The mechanics of how a free attribute available to a transactor will be used under fixed pay or under a share contract are presented in Chapter 3.

engines using premium gasoline are well suited for cabs. If drivers who rent their cabs pay for gasoline, they will gain by using regular gasoline; as a result, the engines will wear out prematurely. Even partners may choose to use regular gasoline. Each saves the entire difference in price relative to what he or she would have paid for premium gasoline while bearing only half the cost of the resulting engine damage. To prevent this, cabs are expected to be fitted with engines that use regular gasoline. Cabs will be fitted with engines that require premium gasoline only if a centralized organization takes charge of fueling them.[4]

Several workers may be required to make a large machine function. If all of them share in its ownership, then the absence of constraints on individual behavior will permit many of the attributes of such a machine to become common property. As a result, incentives for such activities as careful handling and maintenance may be greatly weakened. As will be explained later in this chapter, this problem may be alleviated if many of the individuals who work with the machine become employees of the machine's owner. Not all those working with the machine are expected to be the owner's employees, however. For instance, the machine's manufacturer may have sold it with a guarantee, while retaining the function of servicing it. In that case, contrary to the standard model, some of the individuals working with the machine are not the employees of its (nominal) owner.

Where an office building accommodates many workers, common-property problems such as the use of corridors and access to utilities need to be addressed. Still, most of the structure can be assigned to distinct individuals, and individuals' rights can be reasonably well delineated. The building's users do not have to be severely constrained not to damage it and can conveniently belong to more than one organization. Before moving on to discuss the nature and the organization of office building ownership in greater detail, let me summarize the discussion up to this point.

The preceding examples address common-property problems that arise when the ownership of goods is divided among individuals. These examples also illustrate that the severity of the capture problem varies from one case to another and, indeed, that the severity of the capture problem is not uniform for different attributes of a single piece of equipment. Because different attributes of a piece of equipment are not equally susceptible to capture, it may be advantageous to handle its various attributes differently. Attributes susceptible to serious common-property problems, such as equipment lubrication, will tend to be owned by orga-

---

[4] By the same token, rental cars – even fancy ones – are expected to be equipped with engines requiring regular gasoline.

nizations created to control these problems. On the other hand, attributes that are relatively free of such problems will tend to be individually owned. The ownership of a capital good is expected to be vested in neither a single person nor a single organization. The maximizing ownership pattern of individual attributes of equipment is the one that will minimize the capture loss net of the cost of loss prevention.

Because large pieces of equipment often possess major attributes that are susceptible to common-property problems, they will, according to the hypothesis presented here, be owned by some centralizing organization, an organization that may be called a "firm." This firm may appear to conform to the received firm, enjoying a scale economy in the use of equipment. However, unlike the received firm's product, the product of the current firm is determined by the nature of the common-property problems it encounters. When different attributes of a single piece of equipment are owned by different individuals or different organizations, each will produce its own output. The capital good "large office building" is a striking example of an asset subject to scale economy. Although it is ideally suited to determine the size of the standard model of the firm, its attributes are owned by a number of owners.

Large office buildings are owned and used in a radically different way from that implied by the standard model. The owner of a large office building is the individual or the organization holding the title to it. Nevertheless, that owner does not usually retain the rights to all attributes of the building, his or her ownership being circumscribed. The individuals working in an office building are seldom the employees of the owner of the building, and the owner who holds the title to it is, as a rule, distinct from the firms that actually use it. Indeed, sometimes the titleholder supplies little more than the coordination of the contracts that govern the use of the building between various firms, each of which owns some of its attributes.

The structure of rights over a large office building is complex. The titleholder usually rents out office space, thereby relinquishing to the tenants a subset of the rights he or she has previously held; the renters – the tenants – become owners of these rights. These tenants, which are often distinct firms, produce distinct outputs that have little to do with either the building or its scale. Moreover, other parties are often granted rights to other attributes of the building. If the building has been mortgaged, the mortgage-holding bank has most likely imposed restrictions on the building owner, thereby making itself the owner of a subset of rights. It meets the definition of "owner," since it becomes a residual loser if the landlord, that is, the titleholder, is unable to make mortgage payments. If the landlord has retained a janitorial service, the supplier of that service assumes the liability for its operation and is, in turn, the owner of another subset of rights.

Given that several organizations hold rights over an asset such as an office building, the question arises as to the principle that governs the allocation of these rights. As I have suggested, the structure of rights is expected to be designed so as to allocate ownership of individual attributes such that the parties who have a comparative advantage in affecting the income flow over the attributes that are susceptible to the common-property problem will obtain rights over them.

INSURANCE: A METHOD OF
TRANSFERRING OWNERSHIP

I shall discuss one additional right, namely, that associated with fire insurance, in greater detail than others because the fire insurer's role as residual claimant is easy to grasp and because it seems to counter the perception of the function of fire insurance held by many economists.

It is commonly assumed that building owners buy fire insurance because they are risk-averse and would like to shift the financial risk of fire to those more willing to assume such a risk. I, however, assume risk-neutrality (which is not unreasonable in this case). Risk-neutrality implies that the sole objective of the building owner regarding fire is the minimization of the expected net loss from it. What can explain the fire insurance transaction? I shall argue that one explanation for such a transaction is that fire insurers are more efficient than are the titleholders of buildings as owners of the fire-risk attribute of office buildings.

Not being a fire-prevention expert, an office-building owner would like to secure the services of someone to minimize the expected loss from fire. The specialist could be hired for a fixed wage; however, the owner lacks the proper knowledge to direct the employee to do the right job. Under a fixed wage, the employee would find it easy to shirk and would have no strong incentive to ensure that the fire-prevention program is efficient. It is possible to overcome this difficulty by making the specialist responsible for his or her own actions. The specialist who charges a fixed fee for his services, while assuming the residual claimancy to his actions, is providing fire insurance at a fixed premium.[5] As an insurer, the specialist will lose from fire and gain from its absence. He is, therefore, motivated to take such preventative actions as minimizing fire hazards, conducting fire drills, and enhancing speedy fire fighting when fire does occur, in order to reduce the level – or, more accurately, the net expected cost – of

---

[5] The need for capital to guarantee the actions will be discussed in the next chapter.

fire losses. The insurer is thus one of the owners of the building: He or she owns the fire occurrence attribute of the building.[6]

This analysis of fire insurance constitutes the application of a general principle. As a rule, specialists know more about their line of business than do their customers. They are therefore in a position to charge for service that is of a higher quality than what they actually provide. For this reason people would be reluctant to deal with them were their services not guaranteed. Insurance may be viewed as one form of the sale of guaranteed service. It also amounts to a division of the ownership of the insured assets between the nominal owners and the insurers themselves.

Fire insurance is seldom all-encompassing. Full insurance coverage implies that the insurer is the sole residual claimant of the fire hazard facing the insured firm.[7] It is unlikely, however, that only the insurer can affect the incidence of fire and the loss from it; the insured is also expected to affect fire losses. The latter usually makes decisions about where and how flammable materials are stored, whether or not smoking is discouraged, and how well its employees keep fire escapes unobstructed. Both parties, then, contribute to the mean effect of fire hazard, and both are expected to bear some of the effect. Consequently, coverage is not full and both the insured and the insurer become, to varying degrees, residual claimants, that is, owners of the fire hazard.

There are two refutable implications that could test the hypothesized role of insurance. One relates directly to fire insurance, whereas the other is less specialized. The first states that when a party's contribution to the *mean* loss of fire decreases, the fire-insurance contract will be modified to decrease that party's *share* of the fire losses. For instance, suppose that motors are used in the insured operations. A switch by the insured – due, say, to a change in relative fuel prices – from gasoline motors, which are a serious fire hazard, to electric motors, which are less of a fire hazard, constitutes a reduction in the insured's contribution to fire hazard. Besides the reduction in total insurance payments, his or her *share* in the income variability due to fire hazard ought to be reduced; in this case his or her coinsurance rate should be lowered.[8]

The second implication concerns a distinct pattern of attribute ownership between two types of condominiums. In the first all the units are

[6] The expected value of such ownership is negative; hence the insurer makes a negative payment (i.e., he or she receives a premium) in order to acquire the right to the fire-occurrence attribute.

[7] For coverage to be full, it must include, besides direct losses, such effects as those due to lost business, to inconvenience, and to suffering.

[8] Insurers indirectly perform another service: the policing of employees' diligence in reducing expected fire losses. A relative increase in some premiums signals to owners that their employees have become too lax. For a related discussion, see Hall 1986.

located in one building, whereas in the second the individual units consist of separate structures. Fire and plumbing problems in one unit are more likely to spill over to other units in the single building than among the separate structures. It is expected that in the single building the apartment owners will allocate the ownership of the effects of fire and plumbing problems to the management, whereas the individual owners will tend to own (and, if they so choose, to transact for) these attributes where units are in separate structures.

The argument presented in this chapter suggests that the severity of the common-property problem encountered as a result of equipment use varies from one piece to another, as well as across different attributes of the same piece of equipment, and that the divided ownership of the equipment permits the separate handling of various common-property problems. Each problem can receive individual treatment, while areas from which the common-property problem is absent may entirely escape the treatment designed to cope with common-property issues. The analysis that leads to the notion of isolating individual common-property problems through divided ownership is only the first step toward the analysis of the solution of such problems. To this end, I shall next examine the ways in which people reduce the costs associated with common-property problems.

MITIGATING COMMON-PROPERTY PROBLEMS: SCALING EQUIPMENT DOWN AND USING THE FIXED-WAGE CONTRACT

I have thus far concentrated on the multi-attribute nature of commodities and have pointed out that since not all the attributes of even large-scale equipment are subject to common-property problems, it may be advantageous to make at least some of these the exclusive property of the individual users. In this section I discuss methods users employ to cope with attributes that are subject to common-property problems.

The simplest way to contain the common-property problem in the use of equipment is to scale it down in size and value. If the equipment is scaled down to fit a single operator, the capture problem disappears, the problem of raising capital is eased, and the need for organization is obviated. The sacrifice associated in economies of scale, however, is often too large.[9]

An example of the scaling down of equipment is provided by many of

[9] The potential for multiple shifts is also sacrificed as long as the equipment is used by only one person. This potential is sometimes also sacrificed within firms, presumably to enhance employees' accountability and thus ease remaining common-property problems.

the tools designed for non-professionals. These are often low-cost, low-quality versions of superior professional-quality tools. Professionals can afford the higher prices because they use the tools more intensively. If a rental market were to develop, non-professionals could then use tools designed for professionals. The common-property problem would reappear, however, since individual users would have little incentive to handle the tools carefully. The problem seems severe enough that amateurs prefer to be the sole owners of low-quality tools rather than share the use of high-quality ones.[10]

Another method of containing capture costs, which does involve organization, is the imposition of restrictions on the users of equipment in order to reduce their excessive and careless use of it. The wage contract constitutes a major application of this method. By virtue of rewarding the worker for his or her time, that contract abates the excessive and careless use of equipment. This is an implicit result of the argument put forth in Chapter 3. I noted that nutrients are a free attribute to fixed-rent tenants, who are expected to extract them in higher quantities than would a self-employed owner. Nutrients may be a free attribute to fixed-wage workers as well. Since such workers do not gain from extracting the nutrients, they have no incentive to extract an excessive amount. Similarly, fixed-wage workers who share equipment do not expect to gain from exploiting it, and so would tend not to overexploit it.

Were the wage contract strictly an exchange of time for money, employees would simply provide time without ever lifting a finger as long as work effort did not directly generate utility. Although such employees would not harm the equipment around them, neither would they do anything useful. It is obvious that the wage contract is more than an exchange of time for money; employers must be able to induce employees to perform various tasks at some minimal pace. Given job specifications and the level of supervision, workers are expected to satisfy the requirements at the least cost to themselves. They will necessarily put out less effort than self-employed workers do because, on the margin, employees are not remunerated for effort. Since workers under a wage contract are not paid for output, their incentive to overuse whatever equipment they are provided is curtailed. For the same reason, the wage contract may also be used to control equipment abuse when a piece of equipment is operated solely by one person but owned by another.

Were workers' and machines' exertions proportionate, employers could fully rely on workers' maximization (i.e., doing as little as they can get away with) to avert the overuse of the equipment. Some substitution between workers' and machines' exertion, however, seems possible; at

---

[10]They also enjoy quick access but forgo the opportunity to share the costs of storage and maintenance.

the very least, workers lack the incentive to service their equipment. Therefore, job specifications and supervision must take into account such opportunities and make provisions for equipment maintenance.

Workers who sell their labor services by way of a wage contract are engaged in a constrained transaction: They agree to obey a certain range of instructions. These instructions are designed to induce the performance of productive services and to discourage workers from inflicting harm on equipment (or on fellow workers). In turn, employers also accept various constraints on their own behavior, such as agreeing to a maximum equipment speed, providing coffee breaks, and permitting grievance procedures.

CONCLUSION

Although commodities and production equipment constitute single physical entities, as a rule they have many distinctly different attributes. The value of multi-attribute assets is not necessarily maximized if these assets are owned by single individuals; it may be enhanced by allocating ownership over individual attributes according to comparative advantage. Thus, fire insurers rather than the nominal titleholders of assets are the efficient owners of the assets' attribute of fire hazard because the former rather than the latter are the specialists in minimizing fire losses. As owners, insurers are the residual claimants to fire protection, gaining most by minimizing the net loss from fire.

Some equipment, especially that which is large-scale, may benefit from having multiple users. In that case, however, some of its attributes may be subject to common-property problems. The equipment may be scaled down to avoid these problems. Alternatively, the equipment operators may be constrained. The wage contract removes workers' incentive to overuse equipment by rewarding workers for their time. Many persons may work with a single piece of equipment without treating it as common property. Whereas the received analysis of labor provides no explanation for using time as the dominant unit by which labor is exchanged, the role of the wage contract in averting equipment abuse may partially explain its widespread use.

The labor contract is but one of many contracts imposing constraints on the transactors; such constraints constitute an integral part of any organization. The employment contract and the associated constraints may appear to lead to the theory of the firm. However, as will be discussed in the next chapter, constraints are also common in what are usually called market transactions, and therefore the absence or presence of constraint does not generate a clear distinction between operations in the market and in firms.

5

The old firm and the new organization

For many years the theory of economic organization was nearly synonymous with the theory of the firm. Standard economics textbooks occasionally referred to other forms of organization, such as the family and government, but the firm was the only organization consistently and systematically discussed. Nevertheless, the exact function of the firm remained unclear. Knight's (1921) attempt to add substance to the construct called the "firm" did not fare very well, and Coase's (1937) revolutionary approach to organization required several decades, as well as his own work on social cost, to begin to influence economists. Both of these efforts focused on the firm. In more recent years, Coase's transaction cost ideas have been exploited by economists attempting to generate a theory of the firm, as well as by others who question the usefulness of such a theory.[1] The insights gained through these efforts have been considerable, yet our understanding of organization is only in its infancy. In this chapter the transaction cost approach to organization will be extended.

In order to appreciate the need for the transaction cost approach and its contribution, one must first examine the received model of the firm extensively and critically. I attempt to show that as a description of real firms the received model is untenable, and that under conditions that would allow a textbook firm to exist, its function would become inconsequential. Turning to general problems of organization, I first consider the distinction between market and firm transactions and the significance of Coase's discussion of liability. I then briefly outline the major contributions to the theory of the firm. Finally, I describe in greater detail my own contribution, which stresses the guaranteeing role of equity capital.

[1] Prominent among these are Alchian and Demsetz (1972), Williamson (1975), Jensen and Meckling (1976), Klein, Crawford, and Alchian (1978), and Cheung (1983).

Economic analysis of property rights

A CRITIQUE OF THE RECEIVED MODEL OF THE FIRM

Underlying the received model of the firm is the production function: a relationship that tracks the highest output any set of inputs can produce using the available technology. The firm is simply an organization whose purpose is to select the optimal points on the production function, acquire the necessary inputs, and transform them into output, which it sells. Its objective is profit maximization: in other words, maximizing the difference between revenues and expenses. The cost function, the "dual" of the production function, plays a major role in shaping the firm.[2]

Actual observations do not support the notion of "duality" between the production function and the cost function. Besides labor, equipment, and materials, firms also purchase a host of inputs – including financial, accounting, personnel, marketing and legal services – that are used for "organization" and "monitoring." These latter inputs seem neither to contribute to "production" nor to perform technological functions. Viewing the relationship from another angle, technology does not seem to be the basis of many firms' organizational makeup. For example, it is hard to imagine that technological know-how could be relevant to a firm's decision as to whether it should increase the number of its plants and, when it decides to expand, whether it should build new plants or acquire already existing ones from other firms. The production function is not the "dual" of the cost function if it accounts neither for all firms' expenditures nor for the scope of all firms' activities. What, precisely, does the firm produce? The implicit assumption employed by the standard approach seems to be that each firm performs only one function and that two firms producing the same output (the same Q) do indeed perform the same operations. In reality, most firms perform a variety of operations, not all of which are identical among those firms that seem to produce the same commodity.

Suppose the commodity being produced is cars. Its parts must be produced and assembled. According to the notion of duality, the production function should determine the scope of the firm. It should inform us as to whether the production function of finished cars involves only their assembly, in which case the firm should specialize in assembly, or also the production of the parts, in which case the firm should perform both functions. Engineering considerations, however, seem irrelevant to the question of whether one integrated firm could perform these two sets of operations at a lower cost than could two specialized firms. Indeed,

---

[2] Duality theory relates costs and production functions. Varian (1992), for instance, defines the firm in terms of the production function (p.1). He discusses technology in some detail (pp. 2–22), and states (p. 84) that it is straightforward to derive the cost function given the technology.

whereas one can presume that Japan and the United States exploit the same production function, Japanese car manufacturers are less vertically integrated, buying more parts from other firms, than are their American counterparts. To speak more generally, the determination of whether to perform any function in-house, that is, within a single firm, or to have it performed in the market by separate firms does not seem to depend on technology. It does not seem that the differences among such firms are attributable to production function considerations.

One could argue that Japanese cars differ from American cars, and that the two sets belong in different industries. However, one must be able to specify a priori what constitutes a difference between commodities. Existing theory provides no guidance on this issue. Without such guidance, refutation of the theory appears impossible, since any discrepancy across firms between the production and cost functions may be attributed to differences among the commodities produced by such firms. In this light, duality is not useful; it must, therefore, be concluded that it is contrived and should not be used to describe real firms.[3]

The absence of close relations between the production and cost functions is further illustrated by noting that some firms are housed in more than one plant, whereas sometimes the same physical plant houses more than one firm. The observation that production is organized "in-house" does not imply a strictly technological relationship.

Implicit to the conventional analysis of the firm is the assumption of the existence of costless information. As will become clear in the course of my discussion, this assumption, particularly as it has been applied to the prices and the attributes of inputs and outputs, is the fundamental reason for the discrepancy between the conventional model and actual observations. If information is freely available, then factors' contributions can be easily assessed, and monitoring their performance becomes superfluous. It is not surprising that in these discussions monitoring is virtually never mentioned.

Consider the rewards to factors used by firms and the notion of the residual claimant. According to the conventional model, the owner of the firm makes fixed payments to hired factors and receives the residual from the operations of the firm. That analysis is problematic: The existence of residual in the received, competitive model is inconsistent with the rest of that model, nor is the actual remuneration of other factors fixed in the way the model requires – per unit of output.

The question of how fixed the remuneration of factors employed by the firm is will be discussed later in this chapter. For now let us turn to the concept of the residual. In the Walrasian model, factors of production

---

[3] My critique of the production function is in the same vein as are Goldberg's (1985) and Williamson's (1985).

and commodities are homogeneous, prices are known constants, and the production function is known to all. In that model there are no random factors and no residuals. Knight (1921), apparently the first to consider the entrepreneur as a residual claimant, did not indicate how a residual enters the model of the firm. Random forces are one possible source. For instance, changes in the weather produce shifts in the costs of and perhaps in the demand for agricultural products. Such shifts yield new equilibriums and correspondingly result in changes in the prices and quantities of factors and products. Nevertheless, under the specified conditions, factor-payment must exhaust the product; there can be no "residual." In any case, Knight was primarily concerned not with factors such as the weather but, rather, with human forces that contribute to uncertainty. The received competitive model, however, does not appear to be capable of accommodating such unexpected discrepancies between revenues and costs. I suggest that the costliness of information can generate residuals.

Specification of the precise units by which inputs are employed receives almost no attention in standard texts, yet in reality such units are diverse. In the case of labor, inputs are sometimes measured by time and sometimes by performance. Labor service is a major production function input that workers supply. The labor input required by the production function is in efficiency units: A worker who contributes twice as many *efficiency* units as does another worker also provides twice the amount of labor input. In a similar vein, the demand for labor is taken as a function of labor's *contribution to output*. In the standard formulation of the cost function, however, labor, when explicitly considered, is not usually entered by units that correspond directly to its contribution. Instead, the labor input entering the cost function is measured by the hour, and so labor is accounted for in units of time. Hours can readily substitute for efficiency units only if the relationship between the two is proportional. Because workers themselves are maximizers, it seems highly plausible that inducing workers to apply their time efficiently requires supervision. Moreover, supervision costs are unlikely to be proportional to labor costs under all circumstances; as conditions change, therefore, the per-hour efficiency of labor is also likely to change. Proportionality is unlikely to be present. The question of whether to employ labor by the hour or to pay on a piece-rate basis becomes relevant here, but it cannot be dealt with by the conventional model.

The use of the hour as the unit of labor input in cost functions is not justified by standard production function considerations, and it is improper to switch from one function to the other unless information and supervision problems are taken into account. The reason hours are nevertheless used in cost functions seems to be simply that the dominant mode of employing labor happens to be by time, and the assumption of proportionality between actual hours and efficiency units is made in order that hours may be employed in production function analysis.[4]

The need for supervision arises because the factors contributing to a firm's production are not all owned by the same person. The ownership pattern of factors used by the firm is seldom explored in the received analysis, even though the typical implicit ownership assumptions are not innocuous. Firms are assumed to own the capital equipment they use and to hire labor. Hiring labor means renting labor services from the owners of the capital good "labor." In a non-slave economy, workers allow firms to use some of the services the capital good can generate. If firms choose to own their capital equipment rather than rent it, one must conclude that rental is more problematic than ownership; it is plausible, then, that the use of labor is similarly problematic. In reality, firms do not own all the capital they use; capital is also partly rented. To the extent that firms are financed by borrowing, they are renting rather than owning the capital. Moreover, firms often rent space and equipment. It is not self-evident that those firm owners who borrow or rent capital and who employ labor have interests that coincide with the interests of the owners of the rented assets as to how these assets should be employed. As a rule, the question of whether these interests coincide is simply ignored in the textbook analysis of the firm. If assets owners' interests do not coincide, then methods of reconciling them must be considered.[5]

Returning briefly to the notion of duality, it is possible to write a production function for any process, however complex, even for one incorporating monitoring technology. It seems unlikely that attempting such an inclusion here would be useful. The usefulness of a production function in economic analysis lies in its economy in describing economic relationships. If monitoring were included, this economy would be lost. The inclusive function would depend, for instance, on whether labor is employed by the hour or by the piece, which, in turn, depends in part on the market prices both for labor and for the output. Even if it could be successfully formulated, the complexity of such a function would render it unmanageable, and there is little chance that it could be tested.

It is desirable to reexamine, albeit briefly, the relation between the industry's supply function and the firm's cost. Applying comparative statics to the received model yields the prediction that firm size will increase when the market price of its product increases. The service "use of office

---

[4]It is sometimes asserted that it is impossible to separately measure individuals' contributions to output. Under the given information assumptions, workers should, nevertheless, be rewarded for their aggregate effort and not for their time.

[5]In some texts, particularly those regarded as advanced, the issue is further obfuscated since productive factors are introduced generically, with no recognition of institutional differences among factors.

space" provides a convenient example for analysis. In practice, the precise nature of the product each of the firms in the industry supplies is not constant over time and is not identical with what similar firms in the industry are providing. For instance, some landlords supply parking in conjunction with office space, some charge for parking separately, and still others whose buildings have parking space avoid getting directly involved with supplying this service to tenants by transferring the right to the parking attributes to independent operators. Correspondingly, there is no reason to expect that all existing firms contributing to the market supply will get larger as the market price of the use of office space rises. The structure of firms is not independent of market conditions. Organizations are structured to solve an array of common-property problems, the severity of which depend in part on the price of inputs and outputs. An owner of an office building who had initially offered parking along with office space may choose to sell the parking component when office rents go up. In that case, the size of the firm, as measured by sales or number of employees, may fall. Whereas we still expect the aggregate supply of office space to increase with its price, the size of an individual firm in the industry, as conventionally measured, may fall. It would be premature at this point to analyze the vertical or horizontal integration of such firms. More appropriate is the question of how people contract in order to maximize the value of their resources, which will be discussed later in this chapter.

Is there any advantage to retaining the costless-transaction world? Certainly, exploring such a world may be appropriate for some analyses. It is not appropriate or useful, however, for analyzing the firm. Costless transacting dispenses with the problems of supervision and divergence of interests among collaborating asset owners. In the textbook characterization of the firm, the inputs purchased in the market are assumed to perform the tasks expected of them automatically and fully. This would hold true if the relation between inputs and outputs were costlessly observable, because then input owners could be remunerated strictly on the basis of their contributions. Such costless observability is one of the features necessary and sufficient for costless transacting to exist. Were transacting costless, for instance, the employer could costlessly observe whether or not workers' time was being efficiently used and could compensate workers accordingly. But any other method of remuneration could just as easily be implemented. It would not matter whether the nominal unit of pay were taken to be the wage, the contribution to output, or any other unit; each could be converted to any of the others without slippage. A firm could function smoothly, but the market, where direction is strictly regulated by prices, would perform just as smoothly. If there is to be a model in which firms perform a non-trivial role, it must incorporate the costs of transacting.

In addition to its logical problems, the received model encounters difficulties when it is used to analyze actual observations intruded upon by transaction costs. The cost of perfectly measuring quantities and prices of inputs and outputs is prohibitive. Were such measurements free – and therefore error-free – buyers of productive services could pay for these services in accord with, and in terms of units of, the resulting output. When measurement of output is costly, paying input owners by some observable measure of exertion may be preferable to paying them by a measure of their contribution. Thus, pay is often a function of input characteristics (e.g., dollars per square foot for rental space and dollar per hour for labor). Consistent with Coase's notion of the firm, with current usage, and with the view adopted here, pay by input characterizes a within-firm operation and pay by output characterizes an across-firms operation. The choice between the two types of transaction depends on measurement costs and indirectly on market prices.[6] The firm, then, may expand or shrink in the absence of any change in technology. If this is correct, the one-to-one relationship between technology and firm cost is refuted.

Part of the appeal of the conventional cost function lies in its use of terms that are commonly encountered in practice. As the preceding discussion reveals, however, the correspondence between the terms used in the theory and those in actual use is ephemeral. The entrepreneur is *not* the sole residual claimant because the reward received by those who transact with him or her are not fixed, and because the scope of a firm's operations depends on factors unrelated to the production function. It is difficult to escape the conclusion that the conventional cost function model is ill-suited for explaining organizational (and probably any other) real-world problems.

It is by now a well-accepted idea that evaluating the contribution of a factor to output is costly, and that consequently such evaluations are not expected to be performed with complete accuracy. In the presence of inaccuracies, factor owners who rent out their assets for a given rate of pay will gain by reducing their effort. Under dispersed factor ownership, the transition from the production function to the cost function inevitably involves shirking. Maximizing individuals must take into account the effects of such shirking and are expected to devise methods to lower the associated losses. Therefore, when the evaluation of performance is

---

[6] Of the three contract types discussed in Chapter 3 in conjunction with farm tenancy, only that of sharing is output-based. Both the fixed-rent and the fixed-wage contracts are input-based.

costly, the choice of contracts among cooperating factors becomes significant.

Both Coase (1937) and the traditional approach group interactions among people in two categories: those carried out in the market and those carried out within the firm. In neither case is the classification exhaustive, but in both cases each of the two types of interaction seems important alone and stands in sharp contrast to the other. In both cases activities within firms, unlike activities in the market, require organization.

According to the traditional approach, entrepreneurs buy inputs in the market and transform them into output, which is then sold in the market. As I have pointed out, under the assumption that firms or entrepreneurs possess perfect knowledge of market conditions, of all attributes of inputs and outputs, and of the production function, organization within a firm is innocuous. Any operation that workers or other resource owners accomplish within the firm is, in essence, an exchange that could just as easily be performed in the market without recourse to such organizations. Precisely the same results that are obtained by firms can be achieved without recourse to such organizations. For instance, any worker may operate independently, remunerated strictly by the value of output (from which damage to equipment owned by others is netted); since the true value of any component of a worker's contribution can be costlessly assessed, the worker can also be directly remunerated for it. There is no compelling reason for workers to become employees, rewarded indirectly by the hour. It is true that there is no harm in employing workers by the hour, because under given conditions their hourly contribution can also be evaluated costlessly. But, as was previously stated, this equivalence between workers' employee status and independent status is precisely what renders such organization innocuous.

Coase adopts a radically different approach in attempting to explain why some activities are in the market, guided by prices, while others are in the firm, guided by orders. He argues that transacting in the market incurs the cost of discovering the appropriate prices and that operating within firms, where the employer has the right to order the employees and to restrict their actions, is a means of reducing the costs.[7] Coase does not follow through fully on his own assertion that market transactions

---

[7] Coase does not explain how employers acquire the knowledge underlying their orders. Since such knowledge must be based on prices, employers' action does not obviate the need to discover prices.

The old firm and the new organization

are costly. In order to incorporate such costs into the analysis, a precise definition of the term "market transactions" must first be provided.

Two distinct definitions of market transactions are seemingly consistent with the common understanding of the term. One is that they are properly and fully priced transactions and therefore free of distortions. In other words, in such transactions individual buyers and sellers bear the full costs of their actions. Whereas Coase does not explicitly suggest that transacting in the market involves deadweight losses, the asserted costliness of such transactions *must* imply that some marginal equalities of the zero transaction cost model are violated.[8] This view of market transactions implied by Coase seems to me to be a correct view of reality. Indeed, it is my contention that the Pareto conditions for efficiency are violated in every transaction.[9] It does not seem useful, then, to define market transactions as those free of distortion if that set is empty.

The other, not well-recognized, definition of market transactions is that, once concluded, such transactions leave no obligations remaining between transactors, that is, these transactions are governed by caveat emptor. This definition of market transactions is attractive not only because price alone affects buyers' decisions but also because of its precise correspondence with a useful and clear-cut practice. However, caveat emptor transactions are costly and govern only a small fraction of the total volume of trade. Although it is attractive, this definition of market transactions is often in conflict with the current indiscriminate use of the not uniquely defined term. When using the term, it is necessary to make clear one's intended meaning and to stay alert to the pitfalls of current usage.

It is useful to relate the notion that market transactions leave no obligations between the transactors to Cheung's (1983) analysis of the firm. Cheung points out that the organizations falling under the label "firm" are diverse; that the wage contract does not sufficiently characterize them; and, most important, that there is no satisfactory operational definition of the term. He suggests that economists should abandon the firm as a vehicle of their analysis and instead should focus on contracts. Nevertheless, Cheung retains the distinction between firm transactions and market transactions. He says that the " 'firm' is . . . a way to organize activities under contractual arrangements that differ from those of ordinary product markets" (p. 3). Given costly transacting, organizing activi-

---

[8] Note that because of the costs of conducting market exchanges, the net amount the seller receives is less than the total amount spent by the buyer: Money prices convey only partial information about the terms of exchange.

[9] The view that, aside from occasional "externalities," markets are free of distortion is pervasive. I believe that this view is at the root of all sorts of confusion, especially when particular distortions are considered to be exceptions and therefore to call for exceptional measures, whereas in reality they are instances of the general case.

ties in the product market – at least non–caveat emptor transactions – may require imposing restrictions on the transactors, restrictions that are of the same character as those in the firm.

Since caveat emptor transactions are costly, they are used only under narrowly circumscribed conditions. Would-be buyers of commodities whose sale is subject to caveat emptor will not part with their money before either inspecting the commodities sufficiently to convince themselves that they are not throwing their money away or, alternatively, satisfying themselves of the sellers' reputation, which requires that the sellers have previously invested in that reputation.[10] Transactions in which sellers incur obligations (i.e., guarantees) are an alternative to caveat emptor transactions; such transactions are, however, accompanied by restrictions on the transactors. The within-firms transactions, then, are not unique in imposing restraints on the participants.

In most transactions, particularly those which are highly valued, the sellers' obligations continue after the sale is completed. This is the case when sellers guarantee sales and when they become liable for product malfunction. Indeed, these two types of obligation often apply simultaneously, highlighting the fact that different attributes of a transaction are subject to distinct problems and are differently constrained. These obligations are parts of contracts that specify what each of the parties agrees to cede to the other. Contracts may also restrain the parties in order to enhance their ability to meet those contract obligations that are not discharged at transaction time. The use of constraints means that price is not the sole means of allocating resources. Implementing and policing constraints require an organization, and different kinds of constraints require correspondingly different organizations. Cheung's suggestion that we study the contracts governing what are considered to be firm operations should be extended to include all constrained operations, whether they are in the firm or in the market.

The employment contract, wherein a worker agrees to be ordered by his or her employer, is the one Coase singled out as characterizing the firm. This contract, however, is just one of an array of methods of constraining transactions. In the discussion of the tenancy contract in Chapter 3, I showed why the share contract and the fixed-rent contract are no more in the market than is the wage contract, even though only the latter is said to identify a firm's operations. Many other contracts do not seem to fall neatly within any single category. Consider the services one secures from an automobile mechanic, a doctor, or a plumber. Contracts for such services take at least two basic forms. In one the charges are by units

---

[10] Strictly speaking, even a transaction solely guaranteed by reputation is not a pure, instantaneous market transaction, since the other side of such a transaction is the *future* retaliation against the owner of the reputation.

of the desired output: flushing a radiator, treating a sprain, or fixing a leak. Charging on this basis seemingly places the transaction in the market. The other type of contract, however, seems to be an employment contract since it charges by the providers' time. These contracts place such transactions in firms, albeit very short-lived ones. Pigeonholing transactions as being in the market or within the firm proves not to be very illuminating. It would be instructive to follow Cheung by attempting to explain the types of contract that may be expected to be employed in different situations. Given the objective of this chapter, however, it would be even more instructive to determine what characterizes contracts that belong in firms and to analyze the structure of firms. With this in mind, the following section begins with a brief description of the existing models of the firm.

CURRENT THEORIES OF THE FIRM

Alongside Coase's (1937) groundbreaking contribution, economic literature offers two additional prominent transaction cost–based explanations for the existence of firms. One is by Alchian and Demsetz and the other is by Williamson and by Klein, Crawford, and Alchian. More recent transaction cost–based insights are offered by several authors. Among these are Grossman and Hart, Hart and Moore, Holmstrom and Milgrom, and Milgrom and Roberts.

As was stated, Coase views the firm as a means to economize on the use of prices. The efficient collaboration of resource owners through the market requires the determination of the prices of factors and of intermediate products at which the parties would exchange. Such determination is costly. Coase argues that organizing production within firms, where the employer instructs the employee as to what to do, saves on these costs.

Alchian and Demsetz (1972) hypothesize that the firm is a means to realize the economies of team production, and that members of the team are bound to the firm by a nexus of contracts. In team production, the output of one member cannot be separated from that of others, but the effort of team members is observable. When the inputs are used within a firm, the firm consists of a residual claimant-supervisor, who is at its center, and others whose output is difficult to observe and who produce the firm's output under a fixed-wage contract, supervised by the residual claimant. Because the supervisor is the residual claimant, he or she is properly induced to maximize the value of the output of the team.

Both Williamson (1975) and Klein, Crawford, and Alchian (1978) suggest that efficient production may require inputs that specialize in their specific endeavors. If such inputs are owned by different individuals, then the parties may be able to capture each other's specific values in the course of attempting to cooperate. They argue that firms tend to integrate vertically because within the organization the rationale for capture, and consequently the deadweight loss associated with it, disappears. In my own study (1982) I also offer a reason for vertical integration. I argue that part of the value of those intermediate outputs that are costly to measure may be captured when their ownership is transferred. Therefore, firms that produce such intermediate outputs are likely to integrate upstream to avoid the capture losses. This explanation of vertical integration is quite similar to, but not identical with, that of Williamson and that of Klein, Crawford and Alchian.

Grossman and Hart (1986) and Hart and Moore (1990) focus on asset ownership. They state that such ownership gives the owner control over all its attributes and makes him or her the residual claimant to the income they generate. By combining the ownership over arrays of assets, the firm saves on contracting costs with individual asset owners. By merging, the firm also gains control that it does not have under exchange between the merged firms. Milgrom and his associates approach the complexity of the incentive structure from a different angle. Both Milgrom and Roberts (1990) and Holmstrom and Milgrom (1994) emphasize the multidimensionality of tasks performed by workers and the corresponding need for coordinated incentives and constraints when the workers operate as employees.

In and of themselves, these explanations satisfactorily account neither for the scope of the firm nor for its boundaries. There appears to be no empirical work that demonstrates that the size and structure of actual firms conform to these models. Casual empiricism does not provide support for the notion that these are the main reasons behind the existence of actual firms. For instance, it is difficult to see how the size and structure of both Safeway and the corner grocery store can be attributed to forming prices, team production, specific capital, the measurement of intermediate output, or the tasks' multidimensionality. Regarding the boundaries of the firm, Cheung points out the ambiguity surrounding what constitutes a firm. He argues persuasively that if we cannot classify activities as firm or non-firm, then there can be no operational theory of the firm. The preceding explanations do not seem to be successful in determining the boundaries of the firm.

I propose that the guarantee function of equity capital is subject to a scale economy that might contribute to an explanation of both the size and the scope of the firm. In addition, this function provides a means of defining the boundaries of the firm. Guarantee problems arise only where variability is present. The allocation of variability must be discussed before the guarantee function can be tied to the firm. It is appropriate, however, to first relate the guarantee function to the Coase Theorem.

THE COASE THEOREM, VARIABILITY, AND LIABILITY

In his momentous article on social cost, Coase (1960) demonstrates what has come to be known as the Coase Theorem: When property rights are well defined and transacting is costless, resources will be used where they are most valued, regardless of which of the transactors assumes liability for his or her effects on the other.[11] In the course of his demonstration, he brings the question of liability to the fore but fails to address the question of the conditions under which liability problems arise. Variability is a necessary condition for liability. Variability can always be eliminated; it can be explicitly priced, or it can be taken care of by sorting commodities into homogeneous groups. Liability arises only because variability is too costly to eliminate. A producer of bottled soda would not stay with his product if he knew that *all* the bottles would explode. A slight but *uniform* defect can be thought of as a liability. Still, the problem such a liability creates can be fully resolved ahead of time by adjusting the price of the product. In both cases, the product is not subject to variability, and liability problems are absent, as are problems of delineating property rights. Despite the fact that variability is present, rights are also delineated when each specimen is priced according to its attributes.

If property rights are to be well defined, the person who benefits another must be fully rewarded by the beneficiary; conversely, the person who harms another must fully compensate the harmed person. By this criterion, a contributor to variability must assume the full effect of his or her actions if rights are to be fully delineated. This condition is satisfied in two of the cases of cooperation between owners of land and of labor discussed in Chapter 3. In one, land but not labor is uniform, and the contract between owners is of fixed rent; in the other, labor and labor effort but not land are uniform, and the contract is of fixed wage. In these two cases transaction costs are not assumed to be zero, but property rights are well defined because the method of pay satisfies the condition that the factor owner who can affect the outcome bears the full effect of his or her actions.

In each of the two cases, rights are well defined *only* because the appropriate contracts are used, that is, the contracts are for *particular* assignments of liability. Were the fixed-wage contract chosen when land is uniform but labor is not, property rights would also not be well defined,

[11] However, costless transacting is a sufficient condition for clearly defining property rights, rendering redundant the requirement that property rights be well defined.

nor would resource use be efficient. The allocation of variability here *determines* whether or not rights are well defined. Therefore it is meaningless to state that if rights are well defined, resource allocation is efficient regardless of who is liable (or who bears the effect of variability).

In general, both parties to a contract can contribute to the variability in outcome. Since the individual effects cannot be costlessly isolated, as a rule property rights are *not* well defined. A fundamental proposition here is that as the effect a party exerts on the value of the outcome increases, rights will be better defined if that party assumes a larger share of the variability of outcome. This is the hypothesized guiding principle behind the formation of contracts that govern the operations of an organization, as well as behind the determination of when a party will assume a larger share of the variability, thereby becoming more of a residual claimant.

THE ALLOCATION OF VARIABILITY AND
THE RESIDUAL CLAIMANT

Each of the operations in which a firm is involved contributes to the income variability to which it is exposed, and each of its contracts with the various parties it deals with allocates the overall variability between them. A party is expected to assume more of the variability, that is, become more of a residual claimant as its effect on the mean outcome increases. Efficiency is the sole motivator for this hypothesis (since the model here assumes risk-neutrality): Parties are expected to assume more of the variability when their gain from affecting the outcome increases, thereby guaranteeing a larger share of their own actions, which could otherwise become damaging. When the parties guarantee their actions, their incentive to take advantage of exchange partners is curtailed.

Consider the variability surrounding the operations of a firm engaged in the production of a commodity. Ultimately someone must bear the effect of every component of the variability in the outcome of the firm's activities, just as someone must bear the outcome of any action. Any activity resulting in variable outcome must have one or more residual claimants. Many input owners can affect the mean outcome of a firm's operations; depending on their contracts, each will bear some of the effect of the variability associated with his or her inputs. For instance, as was previously discussed, a firm that buys fire insurance, as many firms do, is allocating some of the variability it faces to the insurer.

It is conventionally asserted that the contractual obligation employers assume to pay wages to employees insulates these owners of labor services from the effects of variability: Employees receive fixed wages and employers bear the entire variability in firm operations. The term "wage contract" does not, however, connote just a single arrangement: Workers may be hired on a daily basis and paid a spot wage; they may be hired for life for a fixed sum; or they may be hired on some intermediate basis. In addition, the employment contract may contain such features as escalation clauses, schemes for severance payment, and requirements for advance notice of layoffs. The "fixed wages" employees receive are not truly fixed either per unit of output (as duality clearly implies but seldom explicitly acknowledges) or per unit of time. Each of these contracts exposes workers to a variability that differs from that of any of the other contracts. Employers are likewise subject to a variability that depends on the particular contract chosen, because they are exposed to the complementary or remaining variability.[12]

The considerations that apply to labor also apply to both the prices and the quantities of all other purchases and sales. Regarding variability in quantities, firms may purchase their trucks and then bear the effects of varying durabilities across trucks, or they may rent the trucks, shifting the variability in longevity to rental agents. In the same fashion, employers who pay uniform hourly wages to non-uniform workers bear the variability in performance among the workers, whereas workers who are paid by the piece bear more of the variability in their own performance. As a final example, buyers bear the effects of variability in product quality for purchases subject to caveat emptor; if the purchase is not governed by caveat emptor, sellers bear at least some of that variability.

If the function of ownership is indeed to assume responsibility for variability in order to increase joint income, then holders of corporate equity, who are usually passive participants in the operations of their firms, are not expected to become the residual claimants to the systematic component of the variability in the operation of a firm. Rather, an array of other transactors who can affect the outcome is expected to assume the effects of components of the variability. Fire insurers are expected to become the primary residual claimants of the effects of fire; the wholesale supplier of a commodity is expected to sign a long-term, fixed-price contract that guarantees the constancy of the price of his or her commodity, and thus to become the residual claimant to fluctuations in that price; the buyer of bad debts is expected to become the bearer of the variability in the repayment rate. Each of these resource owners who transacts with the firm is expected to become at least a partial owner of the line of activities he or she controls. Similarly, a salesperson rewarded by commission is more of an owner of his or her operation than is one who is paid a fixed wage. An in-house lawyer is less an owner of the outcome of legal action than

[12] Each contract will induce a different performance. The total variability also depends on the contract chosen.

is an outside lawyer paid by the hour, who is, in turn, less an owner of the variability in outcome than is the lawyer operating on contingency.

The model here is testable. For instance, it yields a prediction as to the type of legal services one is to employ. In the case of someone who seeks such services, the more he or she can affect the outcome by his or her own behavior, the greater is that person's expected share in outcome variability. Thus, an explicit dispute about money between a firm and a party it deals with that depends primarily on the legal aspect of the argument is expected to be handled by an outside lawyer on a contingency fee basis, not by the firm's own in-house counsel.

It does not seem possible to state precisely which activities should be designated activities of the firm and which should not. Only when transactions are subject to caveat emptor is the separation between transactors complete. However, caveat emptor transactions are the exception rather than the rule. For all other transactions, contracts impose restrictions on the parties' behavior, to some extent creating within-firm transactions. The strength of such ties is not uniform, and thus some contracts are more within firm than others. Here, too, it is useful to try to determine conditions under which the ties will be strengthened or weakened.

The preceding illustrations of the allocation of variability faced by the firm share a common thread. Each party that sells services to the firm and can affect the outcome of the collaboration is expected to assume some or all of the associated variability. Moreover, to the extent that a party transacting with a firm affects the product it produces, it is also expected to guarantee the outcome to the buyers of the product. Not discussed thus far is the question of why the firm itself would assume *any* variability. The next section contributes to the theory of the firm by addressing this question.

THE FIRM'S ABILITY TO ASSUME VARIABILITY, AND THE ROLE OF ITS EQUITY CAPITAL

In the discussion of the assignment of variability among transactors, I have argued that to maximize the gains from transacting, the net rewards individuals receive must be commensurate with their net contributions. The net contribution is not always positive. It may even be negative, as when one party causes property damage or harms another. The levels of the transactors' own wealth, however, constrain their ability to compensate others when their net contributions are negative. For instance, the payment promised to a factor employed for a fixed rate of pay may diverge at any time interval from the spot market price of that factor. When the reward falls short of the party's contribution, that party must agree *and be able* to finance the difference; when the reward exceeds the contribution, the other party to the exchange must agree *and be able* to finance the difference. The parties, then, must have the means to make good on the guarantees, and people differ in that ability. Because these problems seem most crucial in the exchange of labor services, I will take my illustration from the practice of contracting for labor service.

It might be advantageous for workers to become the residual claimants where their actions could impose a high cost on others. For example, the product they produce might be subject to liability problems. Workers who operate valuable equipment, such as jets, may damage it, or if they use power tools their actions could harm fellow workers. The value of the associated variability, however, might be larger than workers are able to guarantee. As a rule, suppliers of labor services are severely restricted in their insuring ability, particularly since agreeing to use the value of their future labor services as a lien is not legally enforceable: Doing so would constitute slavery. Therefore, although the potential gain from guaranteeing their actions may be large, many workers do not have the wherewithal to effectively do so.

This dearth of guarantee capital can be rectified by trade between the workers who are short of such capital and individuals who possess it. However, the owners of capital will assume the guaranteeing role only if they can also constrain the workers such that their incentive to induce liability problems, to damage equipment, or to injure fellow workers is curtailed; otherwise the guarantee function cannot become profitable. Here again the wage contract and the accompanying supervision may be used.

The capital involved in such a guarantee is "equity" capital. I define the firm by its guarantee capital and by the scope of its guarantees. The scope of the firm comprises *the set of contracts whose variability is contractually guaranteed by common equity capital. The firm, then, is a nexus of outcome guarantees.* This definition is operational. It is possible to determine when the amount of a firm's equity capital that guarantees its operations has increased or shrunk. Moreover, the model can predict when the firm will expand its operations. Finally, the model enables us to determine the optimal debt-equity ratio for a firm – a question that is not within the scope of Cheung's suggested mode of investigation.

Consider a publishing firm. If, for a fixed amount, it commissions a writer to create a manual, then the variability in the sale of the manual is entirely within the firm. If, however, it signs a straight royalty contract with the writer, only part of the transaction is in the firm, since the writer will bear a share of the variability in the sale of the book. Assuming that the latter venture succeeds, and that the publisher proceeds to publish more of the writer's work, the model here predicts that the new contracts will gravitate toward a higher (lump sum) advance and a smaller royalty rate, placing it more within the firm. This is so because as the writer gains experience, his or her work becomes more predictable; correspondingly, the publisher is better induced to advertise the book if the marginal payments to the writer are smaller. Of course, the publisher has many other contracts. Fixed-wage contracts with employees are mostly in the firm, while contracts with salespeople who work on commission are less so. The latter are likely to be even less within the publishing firm when used for sales abroad, where the publisher's expertise relative to that of the salespeople is less than for domestic sales. Publishers' contracts with bookstores may stipulate the outright sale of the books or, alternatively, a buyback of the unsold copies. In the latter case, the transaction partially remains within the publishing firm, since it bears part of the risk of poor sales and, of course, the publisher must have the means for the buyback.[13] Expansion is a final ingredient in the discussion of the publishing firm: If it chooses to expand into an experimental line of publishing, the debt equity ratio is expected to be reduced, since the chance of large losses increases. Before concluding this discussion of the firm, I shall offer a few more observations on the allocation of variability between firms and some of the parties with whom they transact.

Although owners of labor cannot guarantee large potential losses, they can readily finance one particular obligation – to supply labor services when the market wage exceeds the contract wage – simply by showing up for work.[14] Owners of labor are, therefore, more likely to enter into contracts in which they are required to guarantee the difference between their market wage and their actual wage than they are to enter into contracts that require them to guarantee other possible effects of their behavior. The inability to personally guarantee large losses applies to many professionals, including lawyers. For this reason, one expects only large law firms to undertake large contingency cases requiring a substantial amount of legal services without the guarantee of reward in particular cases. Small law firms may be unable to finance the up-front legal services required in such cases.

Owners of productive factors other than labor may also lack sufficient wealth to guarantee their actions fully. Any asset may be used to provide a guarantee. Equity capital, however, is a factor *specializing* in guarantees.

The buyers or employers of any productive factor are able to affect the outcome of the transaction and are therefore expected to guarantee their actions. The better their ability to provide such guarantees, the higher

---

[13] The publisher demonstrates such an ability by simply selling on credit, which might explain why wholesalers often sell to retailers on credit.

[14] In other words, workers simply continue to work at the contract wage, and the difference between that wage and the market wage accrues to their employers.

the value that contracts can generate from a given set of resources. For instance, certain types of workers may be most productive if provided with substantial on-the-job training. Workers may be reluctant to invest in themselves unless their future remuneration is guaranteed. The sufficiency of a firm's equity capital is a necessary condition for it to be able to provide such a guarantee for its employees; ceteris paribus, the higher the outstanding equity capital, the closer to optimal the level of training will be. Equity capital is productive, and its amount will be expanded to the point at which the cost of expanding it by one more unit brings an equally valued improvement in contract terms of the employed factors, including borrowed capital. *The guaranteeing function, therefore, determines* (at least in part) *the optimal level of equity capital.* A firm may be viewed as the set, or nexus, of contracts guaranteed by the equity capital.

The use of equity capital to guarantee the firm's activities is subject to both economies and diseconomies of scale. These scale factors play a major role in determining firm size. The fundamental force leading to scale economies arises from the fact that by its very nature the occurrence of what is being guaranteed is random, and therefore the capital that "stands by" to guarantee one prospect can be used to guarantee others. Put somewhat differently, providing a given guarantee level to a larger volume of prospects requires a less than proportionate increase in the amount of guarantee capital as long as the prospects are not perfectly correlated. This factor, then, favors large-scale firms.

Guarantee capital is not capital itself but the command over it. When a guarantee has to be effected, the capital is transferred from its current owner to the beneficiary of the guarantee. The ease of transfer is important here, but it is costly as well. The guarantor who holds enough cash to be able to effect the guarantee loses the return that an asset would have provided. On the other hand, the guarantor who holds physical capital will incur a cost of transfer when effecting a guarantee; as the size of the payment increases, the cost rises per dollar of transfer, since the assets that must be used for the transfer are progressively less liquid. Although the guarantor is assumed to be risk-neutral, because of this liquidity problem he or she is expected to act as if risk-averse.

Diseconomies of scale to guarantee capital arise when different individuals take part in assembling it. If individuals simply guarantee each other's prospects without constraint, then the incentive for caution is weakened. They may pool their capital, as is done in stock corporations, thereby resolving the free-ride problem. But when individual shares are small, ownership and control tend to diverge. In either case, this problem limits the size of the equity capital and, consequently, firm size.

One final point worth mentioning is that the role of equity capital may be usefully contrasted with that of the share contract. The equity firm uses its equity capital to guarantee its contracts with resource owners who sell their services to it. Under the share contract, the cooperating resource owners simply divide whatever the outcome of their efforts turns out to be, thereby eliminating the problem of guaranteeing factor remuneration. Sharing is likely to emerge when the provision of guarantees among factors is difficult (as is the case when the cooperating factors consist mostly of workers) and when their output is easy to divide. The contingency contract is a form of sharing common in legal work. Under this contract no guarantee capital is needed, but the supplier of legal services must be able to self-finance the legal work since remuneration is not guaranteed.

CONCLUSION

The received model – in which firms are essentially a production function phenomenon and the minimum point of the average cost function determines the competitive firm size – is unsatisfactory. If transaction costs were zero, such firms could arise but would be of trivial importance. In any case, there seems to be virtually no correspondence between such firms and those actually observed. Following Coase (1937), I suggest that firms, or at least organizations, result from positive transaction costs.

Contractors must agree on a formula to allocate the outcomes of their interactions. When such outcomes are variable, the contractors allocate the variability among themselves. I have argued that such allocation is at the heart of organization. The central principle underlying an organization is that the greater the inclination of a transactor to affect the mean outcome, the greater the claim on the residual the transactor will assume. Most activities are subject to many sources of outcome variability, and different resource owners or sets of owners may assume different parts of the variability. Guarantees are required in the presence of variability. Not all resource owners possess the requisite amount of capital to guarantee their actions. This is especially true for those whose main asset is human capital. The owners of equity capital cooperate with capital-poor owners. The former guarantee the contracts of the various other resource owners within a single organization and may be viewed as the owners of the corresponding firms. Equity capital is subject to both economies and to diseconomies of scale. These help determine the size of the firm.

6

The formation of rights

Having analyzed the causes that allow properties to be kept in the public domain, I can now address the issue of the formation of economic (though not necessarily legal) rights. It might be tempting to trace the pattern of currently existing property rights holdings to its point of origin to determine how and why it came about, yet such an effort would be futile. The ability to consume commodities, including those necessary to sustain life, implies the possession of rights over them. Once this is understood, it becomes clear that one cannot expect to discover any evidence of a pre–property rights state, since it is not possible to endow a pre–property rights state of affairs with meaning. In order to gain a toehold on the evolution of property rights, one must start with the simultaneous emergence of life and property rights and then consider a world where some rights are already in place. One must resort to something less dramatic than, but similar to, the physicist's big-bang theory. Once some rights are already in existence, it is possible to explore their evolution with respect to changes in economic conditions and legal constraints.

Inferences about the creation of property rights may be drawn by studying instances of anarchy or violent upheaval that necessitated radical acts of rights redefinition. A spectacular example is that of the California gold rush, described and analyzed in detail by Umbeck (1977). Rich deposits of gold were discovered in California in 1848 when the region was under U.S. military occupation, just days before the signing of the peace treaty between the United States and Mexico. The gold-bearing land was not privately owned, and according to the treaty it became the property of the U.S. government. The United States finalized the transfer of power from Mexico to itself by abolishing the Mexican law pertaining to mining rights on government land, but it failed to enact a law regulating the private acquisition of rights to mineral land until 1866. Although the U.S. government was the nominal owner of the gold-bearing land, it lacked sufficient power to enforce its ownership or maintain order. This impotence was exacerbated in that the thousands of fortune seekers who descended on the Sierra foothills to prospect for gold during this time of anarchy included many members of the American military who had been stationed in California and had subsequently deserted their posts. The gold prospectors were on their own, since there was a complete absence of legal constraints governing the gold-bearing land in California. Umbeck describes how these prospectors peacefully established rights over the deposits in one mine after another and adapted to new circumstances as they arose.

Although the process of forming rights to the gold-bearing land was not subject to much violence, it consumed substantial amounts of resources. Rights delineation was difficult to effect under gold-rush conditions because of the high cost of gathering relevant information. The situation the gold prospectors encountered was entirely novel. Little information was available to determine the precise criteria by which disputes would be settled and ownership ascertained. Rights that are initially in the public domain become well defined when it is possible to determine who the ultimate owner will be. The conditions of the California gold rush made this determination exceptionally costly.[1] In addition, in the absence of state courts and of the known procedures under which they operated, predicting who would win any particular dispute was difficult.

In spite of its appearance, Umbeck's case is not one of a primordial creation of rights, since it is concerned with the private creation of legal institutions where those previously provided by the state have ceased to be available. In another study (1981) Umbeck is careful to note that as chaotic as the gold rush was, some rights were defined all along in practice, particularly those related to human assets and to personal belongings, which included guns.

A SCENARIO FOR THE EMERGENCE OF RIGHTS

As was previously stated, it is not possible to trace the initial emergence of rights. Instead, I shall sketch a model that illustrates how, out of a Hobbesian beginning, economic and legal rights may have been formed.[2] While not necessarily "realistic," the model is capable of generating refutable implications.

---

[1] In an oral communication, Umbeck stated that casual evidence supports the notion that miners' earnings equaled their alternative wages. If so, the potential net value of the gold was dissipated.

[2] Attempts are often made to describe the "ideal" state. This is not my intent. Rather, I am concerned *only* with how the state actually evolved.

The formation of rights

Imagine an onset of human history in which diverse individuals are distributed over space. They use their strength and wits to survive, to maintain ownership over themselves when not enslaved, and to acquire possessions. There can be no legal institutions under these conditions; therefore, legal rights do not exist. People, however, have economic rights over their possessions. Individuals interact only to do better for themselves. With the passage of time, they accumulate information about those surrounding them. As they become acquainted with one another's patterns of behavior, they begin to engage in exchange. As long as legal institutions are absent, there exists no third party to compel individuals to perform; all exchange agreements have to be self-enforced.

Exchange, of course, permits specialization. In this scenario, it may be assumed that individuals specialize in the activities in which they have a comparative advantage and engage in trade whenever it is profitable. Of special significance is the exchange between individuals specializing in production and those specializing in protection. The exchange agreements must spell out the amount of commodities the producers will furnish and the nature of the protection the protection specialist will provide. The latter requires the *delineation* of the properties that will receive protection.

In this Hobbesian world, the legal delineation of rights *emerges* through self-enforced agreements between individuals with a comparative advantage in protection and those with a comparative advantage in production. The parties enter into such contracts because, given maximization, each of them expects to gain from the exchange. By delineating rights and adjudicating disputes, the protection specialist erects the legal machinery of the territory he protects and becomes the "ruler" of that territory. The legal rights he delineates enhance the economic rights that already exist. Protection, the delineation of rights, and the erection of legal institutions – which are some of the basic functions of the state – are thus seen to be consequences of the quest for private gain. Given that delineation and protection are costly to produce, however, they are not expected to be carried out to perfection.

Hobbes argued that people will install a ruler (whom he called a king) to protect themselves against their own predatory inclinations. Rulers, too, are expected to have predatory inclinations and might covet the wealth of their subjects. Moreover, rulers are expected to be powerful. Subjects, then, will seek protection from the ruler. It seems plausible that there would be economies of scale in the protection of sets of neighbors against each other and against outsiders by the same protector. The ruler specializes in the management of force. Given the scale economies to his operations, protection specialists are likely to become more powerful than each of their clients. *Before* installing a king, subjects are expected to have formed a collective-action mechanism to control him.[3] This is a non-Hobbesian feature of the model.

Constraints placed on the ruler must accompany his installation.[4] One likely constraint is on the size of the force under his personal command; others include the form of his remuneration and the length of his tenure. By employing him only partly on the basis of a residual from the outcome of protection but mostly for a wage, and by also supervising him, subjects will have made the ruler largely an employed, supervised manager of the protection effort rather than its primary residual claimant. Many medieval city-states in Italy imported a ruler (podesta), typically for a one-year period, and paid him a fixed reward. Such controls and remuneration methods reduced the possibility that he could organize a takeover and amass enough wealth to finance it.

It also seems plausible that there would be scale economies in the delineation of borders between neighbors and the adjudication of disputes that might occur. Moreover, the delineation of assets that the ruler provides for protection is complementary with that required for trade, so he is the low-cost provider of the service. To lower the cost of employing him, his subjects are expected to encourage him to provide legal services and to facilitate contract trade, that is, trade that makes use of third-party adjudication. The more standardized the traded commodities, the easier it is to trade by contract and the greater is the advantage of the scale economies to delineation. The more homogeneous an area, the larger the expected state size; likewise, the more standardized the goods produced in the area, the greater the expected scope of the state.

In this scenario, where subjects maintain tight control over the protector, there must be a balance of power between them, along with safeguards to preserve the balance. The safeguards cannot be perfect, however, and external shocks due to such events as foreign conquest or plagues will upset the balance. The likely outcome of an upset balance is a dictatorship. Once a dictator takes over, the state's economy is likely to decline and stagnate. Nevertheless the initial dictator and his successors are likely to cling to power. It is difficult to return to the rule

---

[3] The organization preceding the emergence of specialized protectors as described here seems similar to organizations that have been observed in a number of anthropological studies.

[4] Given the English model that served Hobbes, the notion of a king (and a hereditary regime) seems natural. The city-state of Venice, however, is a better example. Starting its independent existence around A.D. 600 and ending in 1797 with the Napoleonic conquest, Venice seems to be the foremost example of a constitutional, or rule of law, regime that did not turn into a dictatorship. The ruler position in Venice (the dogeship) was not hereditary, and the power of the doge was rigidly constrained.

of law; consequently, we see that history has been dominated by dictator-ships.[5]

THE COMMON-PROPERTY/PRIVATE PROPERTY
DICHOTOMY

Until recently, most economists had not explicitly adopted a property-rights framework from which to analyze economic problems. The earliest and most notable exception is Frank Knight's discussion of social cost (1924). In his analysis of the use of roads he demonstrated decisively the role of ownership in the allocation of resources. In a similar vein, several decades later H. Scott Gordon (1954) analyzed the common-property problem of fishing in international (public domain) waters. After Knight, and even subsequent to Gordon's contribution, economists did not con-cern themselves much with property rights. Economists' infrequent use of property-rights considerations may reflect a belief that such considera-tions are unlikely to produce useful results. Indeed, because most prop-erty does not appear to be common property and, more important, be-cause the transformation of what is clearly considered common property into what is clearly considered private property is rarely observed, property-rights notions as expounded do not seem to be especially useful.

The perception that property-rights considerations are not useful in the analysis of resource allocation seems to stem from an all-or-nothing view of rights. Both Knight and Gordon assumed that property rights are either present and perfectly well defined or totally absent. They neglected the possibility of an intermediate state in which rights are only imper-fectly defined.

The usual characterization of commodities as homogeneous entities, often with only one attribute, makes it easy to conclude that commodities are either owned or not owned, and that there are no intermediate states of ownership. Such a view seems to have been bolstered by the assump-tion that economic rights are equal to legal rights and that the latter are either present or absent. Moreover, the position usually taken has been that property rights are largely – perhaps entirely – created and enforced by government. Correspondingly, it has traditionally been asserted that it is the government's fault that rights are left in the public domain, sub-ject to "open access."[6] Knight and Gordon implied that if the govern-ment had turned roads or fisheries into private property, the associated

---

[5] Another relationship between property rights and the state is posited by North (1981), who emphasizes the effect of clear delineation on growth.

[6] Similarly, it is often asserted that it is the government's duty to fully protect its citizens against theft.

common-property dissipation would have disappeared. This view is easy to accept if one believes that commodities are one-dimensional, either owned or not owned. However, one then wonders why all resources are not always owned. The existence of theft has been recognized as an exception to the view that rights are perfectly well defined. The notion that rights are not well defined *in general* has not, however, been pursued.

ECONOMIC RIGHTS AND LEGAL RIGHTS

The very success of Umbeck's study derives, in part, from the uniqueness of the California gold rush. Umbeck is able to explain the role of violence or, more accurately, the threat of violence when the state's authority is absent. His results, however, do not apply easily to more orderly circumstances. As a rule, in an already functioning society, the creation of rights is an ongoing process. Rights are created in the presence of state authority, which has a comparative advantage over private individuals in the use of violence and tends to discourage its private use.[7] When a state authority is in place, the role of allocation devices other than violence is greatly enhanced. As I shall argue, as economic conditions change, property rights are *constantly* created and abandoned; therefore there is a need for an analysis that fits continuing, smooth changes in conditions.

It is useful here to reiterate the definition of economic property rights offered in the introductory chapter. These defined an individual's "economic rights" over an asset as *the individual's ability to directly consume the services of the asset, or to consume it indirectly through exchange.* The delineation of property rights is itself subject to individuals' optimization. Describing what the property is and protecting it consume resources, and perfect delineation is prohibitively costly. Hence property rights are never perfectly delineated. Moreover, transacted commodities have many attributes, and the rights to different attributes of a given (physical) commodity or to different attributes of a transaction are not all equally well defined.

Legal rights, as might be expected, are a major factor in terms of their effect on economic rights. "Legal rights" are defined as *what the government delineates and enforces as a person's property.* By granting legal rights, the government participates in defining and protecting economic rights. Legal delineation is likewise both costly and incomplete. Moreover, individuals have a comparative advantage over the government in various delineation activities and actually undertake many of them. Correspondingly, individuals' behavior must be considered in the study of rights formation.

---

[7] Ellickson (1991) shows how rights may be established within existing states, but without recourse to third-party enforcement.

The formation of rights

Rights that are explicitly delineated by the state constitute only a small fraction of all legal rights. The rest are delineated contractually by their owners in the process of exchanging them. In a contract transaction, the buyer becomes the legal owner of the commodity sold by the seller where the contract (often supplemented by common law) delineates the attributes of the commodity. For example, a buyer of a ticket to a play is legally entitled to certain services delineated on the ticket. Contracts, however, seldom if ever delineate all the attributes of the transaction. The buyer becomes the *economic* owner not only of the attributes the seller legally agrees to deliver but also of others where, because of factors such as reputation, the seller chooses to deliver even though he or she is not legally obliged to do so. In the case of a play, the ticket holder has no legal recourse in case of a shoddy performance, but he or she knows that the theater company is likely to do a good job nevertheless. When buying the ticket, the buyer here becomes the claimant to and therefore the *economic* owner of the *expected* level of performance.

To clarify further the distinction between economic and legal rights, let us consider inventions. Many inventions, especially minor ones, are developed into salable products without any legal protection. The owners of other inventions simply do not seek legal protection because the cost of acquiring and exercising such protection is greater than the gain they would generate. Still, inventors often gain from their unpatented inventions, at least for a short span of time. Although these inventors lack legal rights over their inventions, they have economic rights over them. To pursue the distinction further, consider the afterlife of patented drugs. A drug patented in the United States is legally protected for seventeen years. Here, as in the general case, the legal rights tend to enhance the economic rights. When the patent for a drug expires, generic competitors often emerge. Nevertheless, the originally patented drugs typically sell at a large premium relative to the generic ones. In spite of the loss of legal protection, inventors retain substantial economic rights over their drugs. The reason seems to be that many buyers find it too costly to ascertain the properties of the generic medicines and are willing to pay a premium for the established brand-name ones. The rights the inventors retain result from consumers' *ignorance*.

THE DELINEATION OF NEW RIGHTS

The seed for the analysis of rights creation in an ongoing society was planted in Demsetz's (1967) study of the Montagnais Indians of Labrador. Demsetz's point is so simple that it now appears to be self-evident: New rights are created in response to new economic forces that increase the value of the rights. According to this view, rights in the sense of the ability to gain from property are largely a matter of economic value rather than legal definition. Demsetz hypothesized that as the value of a common-property resource increases, people are more likely to establish rights over it. Specifically, he noted that prior to the Europeans' arrival in Labrador, when the value of beaver pelts was low, beaver habitats were held as common property. When the European market became accessible, the value of beaver pelts increased and beaver habitats were converted to private property. Demsetz did not, however, explore the nature of the break between the old and new concept of rights; despite the novelty of his observations, he failed to follow through systematically.[8] Though some economists (and other social scientists) have applied Demsetz's ideas, they have not extended his methodology. I have chosen to expand and elaborate on this embryonic analysis of the formation of rights in order to show how individuals tend to delineate rights routinely more carefully as the value of these rights increases and less so as their value declines.

People acquire, maintain, and relinquish rights as a matter of choice. For example, after the discovery of gold in California, individuals found it worthwhile to delineate very accurately their rights to certain gold-bearing properties. After extracting only the relatively easily mined gold, they often chose to abandon their claims. Individuals take such actions directly in the private sector and indirectly, through the state, in the public sector. People choose to exercise rights when they believe the gains from such actions will exceed the costs. Conversely, people fail to exercise rights when the gains from owning properties are deemed insufficient, thus placing or leaving such properties in the public domain. What is found in the public domain, therefore, is what people have *chosen* not to claim. However, as Demsetz pointed out, when conditions change, a piece of property considered not worth owning may be newly perceived as worthwhile; conversely, what was at first owned may later be placed in the public domain.[9]

IMPERFECTLY DELINEATED RIGHTS

Assuming that ownership is not attenuated, the legal owners of commodities are free to exercise their rights over their commodities in any (legal) way they choose. What causes an imperfect delineation of rights, then, is the choice of owners not to exercise all of their rights. Since rights that

[8] In the same article Demsetz seems to vacillate between the positivistic view that rights are created in response to economic conditions and the normative view that government should enhance private rights.
[9] Libecap 1989 analyzes common-pool problems in a similar vein. He focuses on the political bargaining for the legal delineation of rights.

are not exercised are placed in the public domain, it follows that people deliberately place some of their properties in the public domain. Two examples will illustrate this point. Both restaurant owners who supply their patrons with "free" salt and owners of movie theaters who charge the same price for better or worse seats, thereby providing the differential free of charge, place some valued properties in the public domain. Patrons capture the rights to free salt by consuming it to the point at which its marginal value to them is zero. Restaurateurs price menu items high enough to cover the cost of the salt; however, they still relinquish the marginal unit of salt to the public domain, since the zero marginal charge to patrons is less than the cost of the marginal unit. Theater owners forgo the differential in value between better and worse seats, while moviegoers capture the right to the better seats by getting to the theater early enough to preempt the occupation of such seats by others, with the value of waiting time of the marginal person in the queue equal to the difference in the value of seats.

Owners are not prohibited by law from exercising their rights and imposing marginal charges for each of their commodities' attributes. Rather, for some attributes they deem the returns to be less than the costs. The costs of imposing marginal charges consist of measuring or metering and policing.[10] Were such charges imposed, the returns for the restauranteurs would take the form of higher prices, net of the cost of the salt, received for meals they provide, whereas the theater owners would be rewarded by higher revenues from ticket sales. Buyers, of course, would have to pay extra for the higher-quality seats and separately for the salt they consume. Still, they would gain more from the lower meal price, and their aggregate net valuation of the movie would still be higher. The owners, however, deem some of their rights too expensive to exercise and choose to place them in the public domain.[11] Since owners cannot capture such values without incurring even greater costs, their actions are not dissipating. Even while seemingly placing such values in the public domain, owners are still able to extract some value. In the case of movie theaters, for instance, owners who sell all seats at the same price have the choice of either preassigning the seats or leaving them unassigned. It is assumed that they choose the method that yields the higher net income, thus reducing loss to capture.

Cases in which owners place attributes in the public domain, as in the preceding illustrations, are ubiquitous. Salt is just one of the many "free"

[10] An additional cost is that of convincing patrons that prices will not be raised after they enter the premises.

[11] A similar discussion is presented in Alchian and Allen (1977); see especially Chapter 5. Because of the cost of exercising rights, the policy prescription that all rights should be made private and enforced by the state is inconsistent with individual maximization and is, at best, innocuous.

attributes available to restaurant patrons. Another is the opportunity to eat at rush hour while not paying the owner a differential above the non–rush hour price, and while capturing the valued rush-hour time, as a rule, by waiting or by rushing ahead of others. Patrons also do not pay, on the margin, for the amount of time they occupy space in the restaurant and for the level of commotion they create. Many similar opportunities are available to supermarket shoppers, who can also capture the value of better than average produce or meat by increasing their efforts at selection. Finally, when renters of equipment are charged by the day, the intensity of use, itself multidimensional, is a free attribute.[12]

When the price people are willing to pay for a service increases, returns from its better delineation also increase. If, for instance, the value of all theater tickets were to be doubled, the difference in valuation between a bad and a good seat would also double; therefore, the return from pricing the difference would increase. Umbeck (1981) pointed out, however, that in the new situation the gain from theft would also be higher, as people would gain more from stealing the difference. They might, for instance, buy tickets for the lower-price seats and then attempt to occupy the higher-price ones. A priori reasoning does not yield the outcome that policing expenditures should increase more slowly than the gains from more detailed pricing. Although owners control which methods to employ for protecting their rights,[13] thieves are also free to use whatever methods they see fit. Thus, the claim that rights will be better delineated when the returns from more accurate pricing increase is not always true.

Although one cannot make unambiguous statements regarding the level of delineation in reaction to the increased value of the asset, one can make such a statement regarding the effect on delineation of a change in the cost of metering or policing. The incentive to steal is a function of the value of the target commodity but not of the costs of metering or policing. When metering or policing costs decline, there is no reason to expect the gain from theft to increase. Therefore, if the costs of metering or policing a service were to decline, rights to it would clearly be expected to become better delineated and the price of the service would conform more closely to its value.[14]

[12] Chapter 3 includes a discussion of attributes that are placed in the public domain for each of the tenancy contracts.

[13] Cheung (1977) provides an example of an unusual policing method. He argues that theater owners in Hong Kong underprice the more expensive movie-theater seats in order to get them fully occupied and that such occupancy constitutes a relatively cheap method of policing. In other words, owners *pay* holders of expensive seats a *fee* (in the form of a lower ticket price) to perform the policing function.

[14] A confirmation of this implication – observing a more detailed price structure when the costs of policing fall – would also confirm that transactions consist of many attributes whose levels vary from one specimen to another; otherwise, one price per class of transactions would suffice.

The formation of rights

Regarding Umbeck's point, shouldn't owners have an edge over thieves or other interlopers? On the contrary, examination of the definition of economic property rights suggests symmetry. Anyone who expects to be able to benefit from an asset, be it its legal owner or a thief, is its (at least partial) owner. When the market value of the asset increases, each of its current owners – and possibly some new ones as well – may capture some of that increase. Consistent with Umbeck's observation, there is no a priori reason to expect that one particular owner will prevail.

Consider a herd of cattle. Suppose that in the absence of theft, it would generate an annual income of $100. The legal owner spends, directly and indirectly, $20 a year on protection. At a cost of $5 a year, however, thieves are able to steal $10 a year's worth of cattle. Given his $10 a year loss to theft and $20 protection cost, the owner's net annual income is $70. The total net income the herd of cattle generates is $75, of which the legal owner owns $70, thieves own $5, and $25 are lost. Suppose that the market price of beef goes up and the potential net annual income from the herd is now $200. There is no a priori reason to expect that the net income of the legal owner will more than double. At the higher value, organized criminals may attempt to steal the entire herd, so it is conceivable that the owner's net income could even drop to zero.

The increase in the income potential of the asset has another effect on the behavior of its owners. It increases the aggregate gains from cooperation among them, which in turn is expected to lead to the better delineation of the asset. In the cattle example, if the thieves were members of nomadic tribes or transients, the gain to the owner of buying them off and subsidizing their settlement in a faraway spot becomes higher. This solution amounts to the implicit reallocation of the rights to the economic value of the cattle. In the process, the delineation of rights over the cattle indirectly becomes clearer. Their gain from theft is thus lowered. The success of such methods, however, requires a supply of thieves that is not very elastic. Similar is the case where a store's merchandise is stolen mostly by employees. When the value of the merchandise goes up, the gains from cooperation between store owners and employees increase, and employees are expected to be made fuller residual claimants to the income they help generate. This may be achieved by changing their status to part owners by using commissions as rewards.

Owners who place properties in the public domain may be able to lower their losses by restricting access to these properties. A restaurant owner, for example, will allow access to "free" salt to patrons but not to non-patrons. The state, too, may restrict access to "free" goods. Recreational fishing and hunting often require licenses and may be subject to catch limits. In some cases the state does not find it worthwhile to impose restrictions. Here there is open access to the public domain, as in fishing beyond states' territorial waters or in consumption of air. Individuals, of course, maximize subject to whatever constraints they face.

DISPUTES AND THE FORMATION OF RIGHTS

Owners of commodities may choose to retain them or to exchange them. Exchange is subject to contracts to which the parties obviously agree. It may be puzzling, then, that disputes over ownership erupt at all. A preliminary discussion of the effects of changes in conditions where delineation is incomplete will reveal what causes disputes and how they are settled.

Commodity owners decide whether or not to place attributes in the public domain. Theater owners, for instance, may price all seats equally one week and then adopt a more detailed pricing scheme the next; they are free to alter which rights they retain and which they relinquish, because they continue to own the asset. The sale of theater tickets constitutes a rental contract of space in theaters, and owners can form new contracts as older ones expire. When owning an attribute becomes preferable to placing it in the public domain, the commodity owner will make the appropriate contract changes at contract-renewal time. However, an attribute that is in the public domain while the old contract is still in force can be claimed only by spending resources.

In the case of theater tickets, the status of those seats that increase in value while the old price is still in force is clear. The advertising of particular pricing schemes for specific durations is part of the contract between an owner and patrons. There is no dispute here between owners and patrons; any breach of contract aside, during the advertised period the rights to tickets at the old price are relinquished by the owners. These rights are not relinquished, however, to particular individuals. Since the value of the seats is higher than it was before, competition among patrons for these seats will intensify. When the value of the seats is higher, the gain from avoiding such resource-consuming competition is also higher; since these rights are already in the public domain, it is not necessarily possible to avoid competing for them.

In the polar cases of a fully owned commodity (or of fully owned attributes) and a commodity placed entirely in the public domain, the commodities continue to be owned and unowned, respectively, when their values change. Disputes, including those that have a good chance of ending in litigation, may occur in intermediate cases. In these cases the contracts between pairs of parties simply fail to spell out stipulations to attributes that seemed to be of little value at contract time but whose value increases before the contract expires. Consider a landowner who rents out a piece of land with a deserted wooden fence on it. Suppose that at contract time the fence, which is not sufficiently valued to be explicitly mentioned in the contract, is simply ignored. Suppose, moreover, that while the contract is in effect, a highly valuable use for the fence lumber is discovered. Because rights to the fence are not well defined, a conflict regarding its ownership may erupt.

Regarding the capture of the rights placed in the public domain, I have asserted that whatever the criteria are for capture, individuals will meet them as long as the gains from doing so exceed the costs. These criteria are set to fit the particulars of the situation. In the case of the fixed-rent tenant whose contract does not constrain the extraction level of soil nutrients, the criterion is the appropriate method and intensity of cultivation; in that of the single-price movie theater, the criterion is time.[15] These criteria, however, do not necessarily remain intact when the gains from capture increase. In particular, parties who initially only implicitly relinquish rights to an attribute to the public domain may claim that they retain partial or complete rights to the attribute and may attempt to compete with their transacting partners in recapturing the relinquished rights.

In the case of a contract that does not clearly delineate some rights whose value has increased, a conflict may emerge. In these contracts the owners of assets relinquish to their exchange partners subsets of their rights to the assets. The initial owners, whose actions (or, more likely, inaction) have implied that they have relinquished rights to an attribute, may now contend that these rights are their own, but their transacting partners may make the same claim. These considerations apply most clearly when the parties operate explicitly under contract; they may also apply to informal contracts and to relationships such as those between neighbors. Consider neighbors who possess a hedge that separates their properties. Initially they may have elected, at least in practice, to leave the hedge in the public domain. Changes may induce them to attempt to capture some attribute of the hedge, however. For example, a rare bird may have built a nest there. Here, too, a dispute may emerge as the value of property previously placed in the public domain increases.

The transactors considered here are operating under a contract, possibly an implicit one. One issue for them to consider is how the court might allocate the disputed rights and what costs they would incur in the attempt to influence these decisions. The parties will compare their predictions of court decisions and of the associated legal costs with those of

---

[15] As stated earlier, theater owners have the choice between leaving seats within a single-price category unmarked or marking them individually. In the former case, patrons must wait for the theater doors to open; in the latter case, they must wait for ticket sales to commence. The latter form favors individuals who are willing to commit early. Owners, then, indirectly decide which type of patrons to cater to.

such other methods of settling their disputes as arbitration or entirely private settlement, and they will select in each case the method they perceive as generating the highest net gain. It is true that the would-be plaintiff in a court case has the power to force the court's resolution of a dispute. When a dispute is actually settled out of court, it is because a would-be plaintiff has perceived this alternative to be of a lower cost than settling in court. The other disputant, however, may provide compensation, perhaps in the form of concessions, so that the method of settlement involving the lowest *total* cost (including the costs of negotiating the compensation) will be selected. Apart from the costs of transacting, the Coase Theorem holds true even here. As is obvious, whatever the parties' decision, it affects rights delineation in their own case. As I will now suggest, the parties' decision may indirectly affect delineation in general.

THE ROLE OF THE COURTS
IN THE DELINEATION OF RIGHTS

The courts participate in rights delineation in two ways. The first is indirect: When the parties choose to settle their disputes without resorting to the courts, their actions are influenced by their perceptions of how the courts would have acted in their dispute. The second is direct: The disputes are actually settled by the courts. The balance of this section considers the second component of rights delineation.

In countries operating at least in part under common law, such as the United States and England, common-law court rulings serve as precedents for new rulings. The courts serve to resolve disputes. When private disputes end in common-law courts, the resolution of the particular disputes contributes to the production of a public good, namely, the delineation of rights in situations similar to the one litigated. Since court rulings become precedents for similar cases, litigants are resolving others' disputes.[16]

Private contractors play several indirect but crucial roles that complement those of the court. One role relates to the gains that result from anticipating and avoiding disputes. Because disputes and litigation are costly, contractors gain if their contracts anticipate potential trouble spots and provide for them. When such contracts do nevertheless reach the courts, court rulings are likely to delineate rights clearly because they are dealing with carefully crafted contracts. This effect is enhanced by forces of selectivity, which partially determine which disputes will be liti-

[16] Private rights are constrained by both common and statutory law. I shall not discuss the forces that affect statutory law, since that would require an analysis of legislative behavior beyond the scope of the present work.

gated. Focusing on the case where parties litigate for direct (mostly financial) gains only, disputants go to court only if they are optimistic about the outcome.[17] Indeed, between them they must err in the direction of excessive optimism. A court ruling that is expected to be too ambiguous to truly settle a dispute deters the parties from litigating. Only if disputants expect a ruling that will clearly delineate rights, thus incurring few added future delineation costs, will they litigate. Among all potential litigants in a given class of disputes, self-selection will bring out the actual litigants who expect a ruling that will clearly delineate rights that had previously been in dispute.

Private contracts affect the delineation of rights in at least one more way. As conditions change, contract stipulations that had been attractive in the past may cease to be useful. Since the common law tends to absorb features that recur in private contracts, it is likely to have incorporated features deemed attractive in the past. The courts are expected to rule accordingly in litigation where the parties have failed to stipulate on various features of their transactions and have therefore implicitly accepted the common-law stipulations. When writing new contracts, however, contractors may explicitly stipulate whatever they wish; as long as the stipulations are not in conflict with basic principles of the law, the courts will respect the new stipulations. As new stipulations are written into contracts, the common law becomes exposed to them, tends to take them into account, and gradually replaces the old, less desirable stipulations with the preferred, newer ones. The common law is continually revised in the direction deemed desirable by private parties.

COMMON PROPERTY

I have stated that economists tend to classify ownership status into all-or-nothing categories, the latter being termed "common property" – property that has no restrictions placed on its use. The term originated in the English villagers' practice of using certain areas for, among other things, collectively grazing their animals and cutting firewood. The current meaning of "common property" certainly does not fit the English villagers' actual practice, as shown by Dahlman (1980).[18] Dahlman's description makes it clear that the village common was open only to the villagers, not to outsiders, and that the villagers' own rights were stinted. They could neither add livestock to the herd nor cut whatever amount of wood they wanted. On the contrary, they were allowed to place in the

[17] Landes (1971) was apparently the first to argue that disputes result from errors of excess optimism. Priest (1980) applied the notion to the decision to litigate, and Priest and Klein (1984) conclusively demonstrated the effect empirically.
[18] See also Ostrom 1990.

herd only a set number of animals, and all villagers were restricted as to the amount of wood they could cut. Whereas that land was held in common, its use was directly controlled by the villagers, partly through voting. It was certainly managed as private property.[19]

Regarding current practices, properties under government control are sometimes tagged as "common" or as being in the "public domain." It is improper, however, to view such properties as being unowned. Properties that in economic (rather than legal) terms are owned by no one are deprived of any value. The view is sometimes expressed that such properties would be positively valued were they diverted to private ownership. A closely related view holds that the transfer of government property to private ownership will necessarily increase its value. A priori reasoning, however, is incapable of demonstrating that private ownership is necessarily more efficient than government ownership or that designating properties such as those in mid-ocean as private will yield net benefits. If, as I have argued, metering and policing are expensive, then private ownership, as compared with a zero transaction costs state, is never free of dissipation. As long as access to, and use of, public property is subject, as it usually is, to restrictions – such as prohibition of hunting of young game animals – one cannot conclude that rights would be better delineated under private ownership than they are under public ownership. The distinction between common property and property under government control will now be examined in the case of the private use of public roads.

Roads are economic goods typically held in the public sector. The conditions that implicitly underlie Knight's (1924) analysis of private ownership of roads are those such that private entrepreneurs can determine and collect the optimal prices and police the use of the roads costlessly. In practice, pricing and policing costs must be considerable. In comparing private and public ownership of roads, it must also be recognized that public roads are not, in fact, managed as common property. Besides restrictions on features such as the safety and size of vehicles, road users are required to pay various fees and taxes, the gasoline tax being the most significant.

The gasoline tax is a device for rationing road use; the higher the tax, the lower the demand for roads and the lower the level of congestion. It is, however, a rather blunt device for optimizing the congestion level. Because the tax payment is proportional to the number of gallons purchased, it fails to distinguish, for instance, between peak-hour use and off-peak use; it makes the wrong distinction, in terms of congestion costs

[19] Dahlman supplies considerably more detail on the management of the common.

users impose, between more and less fuel-efficient cars. However, because of the costliness of pricing and policing, market prices are subject to similar shortcomings. Correspondingly, in their pricing schemes restaurateurs do not distinguish between peak and off-peak hours and between fast and slow eaters. It is incorrect to conclude on a priori grounds, then, that the value of roads will increase if they are made private.

If private ownership is not always superior to government ownership, it is appropriate to consider the hypothesis that efficiency *motivates* placing assets in the public sector. A partial justification for this hypothesis is offered in the discussion of non-market allocation (see Chapter 9). Efficiency considerations will dictate how they are used. It is expected, for instance, that as the costs of, or the gains from, monitoring public-sector attributes increase, the use of public-sector attributes will be increasingly restricted. Testing this proposition will also test the more fundamental hypothesis that the maximizing forces in government are the same as those in the private sector. The following analysis of the delineation of property rights involving the North Sea among the surrounding countries (like the examination of homesteading in Chapter 8) will illustrate the preceding discussion and provide some evidence regarding the operation of government.[20]

THE CONVERSION OF THE NORTH SEA
INTO OWNED PROPERTY

In 1958 the Convention on the Continental Shelf was signed in Geneva (see Dam 1965). The provisions of the convention divided among the countries bordering the North Sea[21] some of the commonly held attributes of that sea, particularly those related to minerals. Two factors had been working to enhance the value of the North Sea in the years preceding the agreement. First, underwater drilling, which was becoming more widespread, was declining in cost; second, various signs were emerging that the region contained natural gas and crude oil reserves.[22] The countries surrounding the North Sea could conceivably have unilaterally extended their territorial rights toward the middle of the sea. Oil companies, however, were not going to invest resources in searching for oil unless they expected their potential legal ownership and, concurrently,

[20] Lueck (1989) demonstrates that state action regarding wildlife is consistent with the hypothesis that its objective is to maximize the value of wildlife.

[21] Belgium, Denmark, France, the Netherlands, Norway, the United Kingdom, and West Germany.

[22] For example, gas was discovered in the Netherlands and beneath the North Sea near the United Kingdom.

their economic ownership of that oil to be secure. The preceding discussion suggests that the increase in value of the oil resources of the North Sea generated forces to better delineate rights over it.

By reaching an agreement, the countries involved gained ownership of segments of the sea. They could then either exploit their sea rights directly or grant them to private parties and let those private concerns exploit them. Subsequent events proved that the formal agreement and the accurate delineation of borders was ultimately of great value. When the North Sea countries convened to establish rights over the sea, no one knew where oil would be found, so it was easy to arrive at a formula that would give each country the territory nearest to it without generating much dispute regarding the precise setting of borders. The formula actually selected was that any point on the sea (and on the sea bottom) belonged to the country to which the point was closest.

As it turned out, many of the major oil and gas discoveries lay close to the border between the Norwegian and the United Kingdom sectors. Since the border was precisely marked, ownership of these finds was not in dispute. There is little doubt that without the agreement oil companies would not have searched in that area. The value of the clear delineation is further illustrated by the following observation. There is a deep trench in the Norwegian sector of the North Sea. Laying a pipeline across the trench is prohibitively costly. Some of the Norwegian oil deposits are on the United Kingdom side of the trench, which seems to make the United Kingdom a more natural owner of that area than Norway. Consistent with the Coase Theorem, however, once rights were delineated, there was little difficulty in developing the area. Indeed, some of the Norwegian oil is shipped by pipeline to the United Kingdom.

MEANS OF ENHANCING RIGHTS

One reason attributes are placed in the public domain is that it is too costly to measure and police all the attributes of a transaction. Transactors may attempt to capture attributes that are not adequately measured, or they may engage in excess measurement in order to reduce capture costs. In order to maximize the gain from exchange, transactors are expected to seek ways to curb such costs. One such method is to exploit scale economies in measuring; another is to discourage duplicating measurements.

Some measuring and policing costs increase less than proportionately to the number of units in a transaction. For instance, as a rule, less unit measurement is necessary when all transacted units are obtained from a single manufacturing batch or from a given field than when they are obtained from several batches or from different fields. Similarly, when a capital asset is rented, the unit cost of measuring the reduction in the value of the asset declines as the rental period gets longer, since these costs are independent of the length of the rental period. Determining how productive the asset is requires only one measurement of the output; determining how intensely it has been utilized requires just a pair of measurements – one at the beginning and one at the end of the rental period. The availability of such scale economies, with regard to both a transaction's size and its duration, reduces the costs of rights delineation and, therefore, the loss otherwise associated with placing attributes in the public domain.

An entirely different method of lowering the costs associated with placing attributes in the public domain is to induce the parties to act as if the attributes were owned even if they are not. When supermarket shoppers are allowed to choose items such as apples, they are in a position to capture the value of the better apples, which are sold at the same price as the inferior apples. Sellers take deliberate action to make the displayed apples appear uniform. Indeed, were all buyers to choose randomly from the available selection (and given competition among sellers), the cost to consumers of apples of a given average quality net of the expense of choosing would be less than it is when consumers actually do pick and choose.[23]

Here are three predictions that relate to delineation: (1) As rental length increases, the fall in the rental fee will exceed the decline in unit cost, owing to the sheer cost of finding additional customers; (2) the more costly the measurement of the asset, the greater the price decline with duration of rental and the fewer the rentals relative to sales; and (3) the more diverse the product offered for sale, the more prepackaging will occur, and, in addition, the sellers who are more reputable will more commonly engage in prepackaging.

CONCLUSION

By their own actions, individuals are able to control and to affect the delineation of their rights over "their" property. Individuals will exercise such control as part of their maximizing process. Whenever individuals find the existing level of delineation to be unsatisfactory, they will alter it until they are satisfied. In the same sense that individuals are always in equilibrium with regard to their asset holdings, they are also in equilibrium with regard to their rights over their assets. At any given moment, their rights are so precisely defined that they do not wish to change them.

Economic conditions, however, are constantly changing, and with

[23] See Barzel 1982.

them the equilibrium property-rights delineation is changing as well. As rights to commodities possessed by individuals become more valuable, the individuals will delineate these rights more thoroughly. As the value of rights to commodities that lie in the public domain increases, people will tend to spend more resources to capture them and to turn them into private property. Such transfer from the public domain to private owner-ship is sometimes effected by individuals and sometimes by the state.

When the value of rights to those commodities that are in the process of being exchanged increases, disputes between the exchange parties may erupt. The resolution of disputes results in the delineation of the con-tested rights. The courts participate in the delineation of disputed rights, and the common-law courts interact with individuals in such determina-tions. Individuals choose whether or not to go to a common-law court, and they will litigate new cases until rights become, in their perception, well defined.

When the costs of metering and of policing assets or assets' attributes exceed the valuations, such assets or attributes will be relinquished into the public domain and become common property. Such common prop-erty is property people *choose* not to own. Both the English common and government property in general are valued, and their use is constrained; as a rule, they are not really common property.

7

Slavery

By the beginning of the twentieth century, slavery had largely disappeared. Although the institution is extinct, comparing slaves and free laborers and exploring the forces that permitted slavery to flourish under certain circumstances can shed light on present-day institutions. It is particularly illuminating with respect to the understanding of the evolution of the status of women and general policing and ownership practices.

THE SLAVE CONTRACT

Labor services, routinely exchanged in the market,[1] are subject to contract. The typical contract for the services of a free worker transfers a rather narrow, usually short-term set of attributes from the labor owner to its buyer. Slavery, too, may be viewed as a labor contract – one, however, that gave slave owners extensive rights over their slaves. In the case of forced slavery, the contract extended over the slave's lifetime. The voluntary slave contract typically specified a shorter duration and gave the owner fewer rights over the slave than did the forced slave contract.

Forced slavery was initiated by theft – free people were captured and, as the term suggests, were forced into slavery.[2] Voluntary slavery was the result of an explicit contract – a contract to which both parties agreed, presumably in the belief that signing the contract would be beneficial to each. In some cases voluntary slavery resulted when people who had posted themselves as loan collateral defaulted on their contract and lenders assumed ownership over them. Indentured servitude, a form of voluntary slavery, was a direct method of repaying loans. Such loans often served to finance the passage of indentured servants from Europe to America. To repay the loan, indentured servants worked in America for

---

[1] The term "market" is used here and throughout the remainder of this book according to its conventional meaning.

[2] See Bean and Thomas 1974.

a number of years virtually as slaves. The duration of the servitude was determined in an auction in which the winning bidder was the person who bid the shortest number of years of service and bought the loan contract from its previous holder – often the captain of the passage ship. The servant worked out his or her debt to the final lender, usually an American farmer.

The term "contract" normally implies a voluntary relationship, indeed, a relationship from which both parties expect to gain. The term fits voluntary slavery well but is less satisfactory in the case of forced slavery. It is clear that free persons, having been forced into slavery, did not expect to gain from their change in status. Therefore, if the term is appropriate at all to forced slavery, it applies only to the period of time after which the persons had already become slaves. Even then, such usage stretches the definition of "contract" to its limit. Nevertheless, it will be seen that the notion of a slave contract is useful in analyzing the institution of slavery.

SLAVES' SUPPLY OF LABOR

Slaves were extremely poor people. A recognition of their poverty is essential if various slave practices are to be properly understood. The utilization of slave labor per unit of time may be explored through the conventional labor–leisure choice analysis. Figure 7.1 illustrates such an analysis, except that in addition it recognizes the effect of fatigue. It is assumed that beyond a certain point in the working day, fatigue becomes dominant and that the slope of the budget line will become positive; more hours will lead to lower output. A free worker with budget MM will choose to be at point A, which lies on U, the highest indifference curve that the worker can attain. A person subject to a budget constraint MM obtains his or her entire income from the use of his or her own time. A budget constraint $M'M'$ implies that the individual has a daily income equal to the vertical distance between MM and $M'M'$ from sources other than the use of his or her own time. Similarly, $M''M''$ indicates a negative non-labor income, that is, a debt-payment obligation. A positive income elasticity for leisure – a highly plausible relationship for a person whose earning power is low and who is a net debtor – implies an increasing supply of labor as the budget constraint shifts inward. Given such income elasticity, as the fraction of a person's potential labor income that must be used for debt repayment increases, the person accordingly increases the quantity of labor he or she supplies.[3]

[3] The supply of labor also depends on the intensity of work, which is usually viewed as given but is actually a choice variable. I abstract from it here; for a more elaborate analysis, see Barzel 1977.

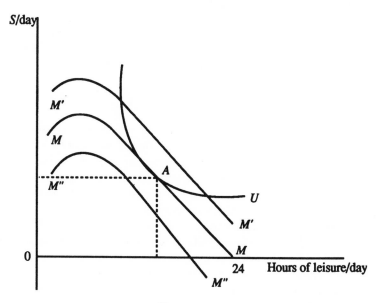

Figure 7.1

Workers incur maintenance expenditures – the minimal expenditures on items (e.g., food, medical care, shelter) that will sustain them at a given exertion level. Such expenditures most likely increase with the amount of labor supplied. Maximum net income from work is the largest present value of labor income a worker is able to produce net of the present value of his or her maintenance expenditures. That particular labor effort associated with producing the maximum net present value also permits the largest possible debt payments. Such a level of exertion defines the largest debt that a person can pay while earning just enough to sustain himself or herself. A free person with a commensurate debt will presumably *choose* to operate at such a level of exertion. Policing costs aside, a forced slave can be viewed as a person who operates precisely at that point. The owner of a forced slave will require the effort that, net of maintenance expenses, will yield the highest present-value income stream. Thus, a forced slave may be compared to a free person who has contracted to operate in exactly the same way the slave is required to. A forced slave is deprived of his or her entire net present value. Such slaves essentially operated under a contract, the terms of which have just been described. It is a contract in the sense that it characterizes the amount necessary for manumission, which is the act of buying out that contract.

In the era when the law permitted slavery, the question of manumission was pertinent. As indicated in the opening paragraph of the introduction to this book, the analysis of self-purchase poses a major puzzle: How could a slave, another person's piece of property, purchase his or her own contract? In order to resolve this puzzle, transaction costs, particularly policing costs, must be considered.

THE COSTS OF SUPERVISION

Since slaves were the full-fledged legal property of their owners, all the income they could generate was legally their owners' as well. Owners who took anything from their slaves were simply taking something that was legally theirs to start with. Owners had the legal right to take; they also had the might. How, then, could slaves accumulate wealth, sometimes to an extent that enabled them to purchase their own contracts? Had both slaves' capabilities and the net output they produced been costlessly measurable, wealth-maximizing slave owners would indeed have extracted every last ounce of productiveness from their slaves. Under these conditions, which would have permitted owners to assume ownership in the most complete sense of the word, it is ironic that slave status itself would have been inconsequential. Had policing been costless, the owner could have obtained the same income while allowing the slave to operate as a free person; for instance, he could have done this by receiving an explicit payment of the same value as that generated by the slave's services without requiring slave status. The free person, however, would still have had to work exactly as a slave would in order to be able to make his payment, or as a debtor would to pay off his or her debt.[4] This is consistent with the Coase Theorem, which states that when rights are clearly delineated – as they are here – resource allocation is independent of the ownership pattern. In reality, the evaluation of inputs and outputs is costly, and policing is required to induce effort. As we shall see, accumulation by slaves is thus possible.

When the net output of a free worker can be determined at low cost, it is advantageous for him to operate independently, since this eliminates the problem of incentive. Such was not the case with slaves; the labor services slaves could provide belonged to their owners. Even when output was easily measured, slaves would have gained from producing less and thus had to be induced to produce more. The distinction between slaves' and free workers' incentives became even more acute for tasks that free workers performed by the hour. Free workers would do best if they could

---

[4]Had all rights been well defined, which requires costless transacting, not only would slave status have been rendered devoid of significance but forced slavery would never have arisen in the first place, since one person would never have captured the rights of others.

convince their future employers that they were more productive than they actually were; since it was difficult to ascertain their true productiveness, their wages would consequently be higher. Slaves, on the other hand, would have done best to convince their owners that they were no good, since little would then have been expected of them.[5] Slave owners, then, had to spend resources to figure out how productive the slaves were and how hard they could be driven, as well as to actually supervise their efforts or output.

Assuming that the supervision of effort is subject to diminishing marginal productivity, in their supervision effort owners would have stopped short of extracting the maximum output of which slaves were capable.[6] The difference between slaves' maximum output and their actual output became the slaves' property in practice. As a rule, it came not in the same form as the product they produced for their owners, but, rather, in the form of reduced effort. Still, slaves were able to convert some of this potential into material goods.

Owners had to choose between supervising their slaves' output, which is comparable to what employers have to do when the free workers they employ work by the piece, and supervising their effort, which is comparable to what employers must do when they employ free workers by the hour. The latter required continuous supervision, for whenever slaves were not watched they had little incentive to perform. The former required overseeing output as to its quantity, quality, and, indirectly, its effect on other productive inputs such as equipment. The supervision of slaves' output also required output quotas; left to their own devices, slaves would have produced as little as they could. Moreover, quotas could not have been set by simply observing past performance, since slaves' incentive to produce little during the demonstration period would have been strong indeed. Quotas were subject to error; too high a quota would have resulted in the destruction of slaves. Owners selected the quota that would maximize their own wealth and were expected to enforce the production of that quota but no more. This means that owners left their slaves with the difference between the quota and the maximum they could produce, a difference slaves could exploit. Given the two methods of extracting output, owners could offer supervised slaves the *option* to work under the quota method, setting the quota to exceed the supervised output. With this as an option, some slaves would have cho-

---

[5] Slaves had to be careful not to do too good a job of deceiving their owners, since owners who thought their slaves were not worth their cost would have found them expendable.

[6] This statement applies to the average slave. Slaves who were mistakenly asked to do more than they were capable of doing were in serious trouble, compared with other slaves, to the extent that they sometimes died of exhaustion.

sen to operate under the quota, since for them the quota obviously was not excessive. Though they allowed slaves to retain output in excess of the quota, owners were aware that the level of the quota could have been increased to begin with. Since owners' confiscation of slaves' accumulation would have been equivalent to breaking the contract, confiscation would have defeated the purpose for which the quota was established to begin with. In pursuit of their self-interest, owners permitted slaves to own and to accumulate.

Slaves seldom became rich. Nevertheless, the free time they were able to gain enabled them, among other things, to grow vegetables, fish and hunt, and also to steal. Their owners and neighbors were ready buyers for what slaves had to sell. Slaves who were ultimately able to buy their contracts were, as a rule, household slaves, sometimes well-trained ones. Because their tasks were diverse, they were difficult to supervise, a difficulty that increased with the skill of the performer. Household slaves, especially skilled ones, had better opportunities to accumulate than did slaves who worked in the fields.

The need for supervision and the desire to economize on its cost made ownership of slaves less than fully delineated. Slaves were able to capture some of these undelineated rights – in this case rights to themselves. Success, partly due to skills in feigning inability, on the one hand, and to activities such as fishing, on the other, as well as the luck of having errors made in their favor, eventually enabled some slaves to buy their own contracts.

SLAVES' CONSUMPTION

The sharp disparity between interests of the owners and those of slaves was not confined to slaves' effort and its supervision; it also affected consumption practices. Owners could not drive their slaves hard unless they made sure that they were properly maintained – that the nutrition, medical care, and other services slaves received were commensurate with the effort required of them. Correspondingly, as Fogel and Engerman (1972) have shown, in the United States slaves received what by nineteenth-century standards appears to have been good medical care and a nutritious diet.[7] Owners, however, had little incentive to let their slaves consume food other than that included in the least-cost diet, or to let them consume other services beyond the lowest-cost ones required for maintenance. Slaves, on the other hand, were not necessarily harmed when their

---

[7] Fogel and Engerman, however, do not interpret their findings on nutrition the way I do, nor do they systematically apply transaction cost notions to the analysis of slavery.

productivity was lowered. Obviously, they preferred more palatable food, which they would have substituted, in part, for less appealing if more nutritious food. One important tool owners possessed for minimizing maintenance costs was the ability to control consumption directly; they attained this control by simply supplying consumption items in kind rather than providing slaves with a budget, which would have permitted choice. Thus, slaves' diet in the American South contained much corn and sweet potatoes, then considered nutritious but less desirable than the more expensive wheat and white potatoes even poor free farmers chose to consume. Owners' control of slaves' consumption, however, was not absolute. Slaves would, on occasion, avoid taking medicine, since in their eyes remaining ill was sometimes preferable to returning to work. Slaves also traded food rations for alcohol on occasion. That providing consumption in kind was intended, at least in part, to restrict choice is demonstrated by the fact that owners not only refrained from supplying alcohol but, most tellingly, also took various costly steps to deny slaves access to it. Drinking reduced slaves' productivity, and owners made a concerted effort to make drinking expensive to slaves.

ENFORCING PROPERTY RIGHTS
IN THE PRESENCE OF SLAVERY

The legal ban on both forced and voluntary slavery is now universal; in earlier eras, various restrictions were placed on both practices. Voluntary slavery was a contractual arrangement into which neither party would enter if she or he did not expect to gain from it, while under forced slavery it was owners who gained. Eventually all states abolished slavery, most of them voluntarily. Needless to say, slaves had little direct influence on the abolition decision. Issues of theft may have been partly responsible for the abolition decision. Because of theft, the institution of slavery, both voluntary and forced, may entail costs that impinge on free persons, who might consider them excessive.

Two forms of theft are associated with the institution of slavery. Already mentioned is the fact that theft was the initial step in forced slavery. The other form of theft occurred when slaves escaped; the escape turned what were to their owners valuable assets into assets deprived of some or all of their value. The loss that owners incurred due to abolition must be weighed against the policing costs associated with theft.

Coercion of free people into becoming slaves has largely been a consequence of raids and of full-fledged wars among nations. For centuries West Africa was subject to raids and was the main source of slaves for the American South, the Caribbean, and South America. Since losers of wars and raids were not the winners' countrymen, one would not expect states to outlaw that source of slavery. However, raids in which free persons are captured and turned into slaves against their will can also occur within a country. Free persons will take steps privately to protect themselves against enslavement; they will also use the state to enhance their rights. The most obvious use of the state machinery is to make enslavement of one's countrymen a crime. A more extreme step is to prohibit slavery altogether.[8] Enslaved persons would have found it exceedingly difficult to demonstrate that they were forced into slavery in a society that permitted slavery. The returns from such theft, then, are higher where slavery is permitted than they are where slavery is prohibited. Conversely, the threat to free persons of being turned into slaves is relatively low in countries that prohibit slavery.[9] The fear free people have of being turned into slaves may partially explain the ban on slavery.[10]

A different kind of cost arises in the case of escaping slaves. It seems to be generally true that certain costs of protecting property from theft are assumed by the state. In Chapter 8, I suggest as a general proposition that activities will be banned if the police protection they require is very costly. If, as compared with the private value of slavery to slave owners, the cost to the police of recovering escaped slaves was excessive, slavery would be banned.

The higher the danger to a country's residents of being forced into slavery, and the higher the cost of recovering escaped slaves, the more likely it is that slavery will be prohibited. For a long time in the American South, being a slave and being black were almost synonymous.[11] Free people, nearly all of them white, did not have to fear becoming enslaved, and escaped slaves could readily be identified and captured. As the population of free blacks grew, however, the distinction between a free person and a slave became more difficult to establish.[12] Consequently the costs

---

[8] Consistent with this view is the observation that raids to acquire slaves declined after the colonization of Africa. Enhancement of property rights within colonies increased the colonies' value to the colonizers.

[9] Isolated cases of slavery are nevertheless reported in the press.

[10] According to Jewish law, Jews were allowed to keep other Jews as slaves. The law required, however, that all Jewish slaves be freed by the onset of every Sabbatical year. If during a Sabbatical year one spotted a Jewish slave, it was clear it was illegal. This constraint on slavery reduced the gain from illegally enslaving other Jewish individuals, and it is consistent with the hypothesis presented in this study.

[11] The identification of slaves with a particular people is the apparent source of the term "slave." To the Slavs the term "Slav" apparently meant "person." Most of the Slavs present in ancient Rome were slaves, and the Romans used the term meant for one to identify the other.

[12] Southern states imposed various restrictions on manumission, perhaps in order to prevent the formation of enclaves of free blacks. These efforts were not entirely successful.

of slavery increased, and the net gain from the institution declined.[13] If slavery were legalized in our own society, the distinction between free people and slaves would be more difficult to establish and the problems of the forced enslavement of free people and of capturing escaped slaves would become even more acute than they were in the Old South. It is not surprising, then, that in many societies slavery was severely restricted and that it is now universally prohibited.

The demise of indentured servitude may have been due to forces similar to those that led to the demise of slavery. At its inception, the population in America was sparse, and servants, at least from Germany, were easily distinguished from free people. Over time, the population grew and diversified, making escape easier and perhaps also making the enslavement of free people easier, thus lowering the net benefit of the institution to the originally free population.

By the end of the nineteenth century, slavery had largely been abolished, perhaps because the costs of policing the institution exceeded its rewards.[14] The current prohibition of slavery implies that each individual is the owner of the capital asset embedded in himself or herself. The abolition of slavery was accompanied by the transfer of such capital assets from the previous slave owners to the slaves themselves. The prohibition of slavery also entails additional restrictions on contracting: Essentially, when workers contract for the supply of their own labor services, only short-term contracts are legally enforceable. These additional restrictions may also reflect the attempt to make the theft of people more costly.

CONCLUSION

Even though forced slaves seem to have been stripped of any rights, in practice ownership over them was not complete. Owners had to spend resources on supervising the work effort and consumption pattern of their slaves and on preventing their escape. Such efforts were subject to increasing costs, and attempts to economize on these costs included granting slaves various rights. In some cases slaves' output rather than their effort was supervised. The attempt to lower the cost of supervision then included granting slaves the right to part of the output or of their own time. These slaves, though legally their masters' property, were able to accumulate wealth and occasionally to buy their own contracts.

[13] Some slaves who were, in fact, freed by their owners chose to retain the legal status of slave, presumably to retain the owners' protection and to reduce the chance of being forced back into slavery.

[14] The institution resurfaced under a new guise in the nineteenth century, with the importation of Chinese workers, a newly distinct set of people, for railroad construction. Like its predecessor, it did not last long.

8

Wealth-maximizing constraints on property rights

The economists who first adopted the property rights framework in their analyses often considered any government restrictions on those rights ("attenuation of rights") to be undesirable. A person's ability to realize the potential value of his or her property depends on the extent of his or her property rights, which consists of the ability to use (and exclude), to alienate, and to derive income from the property. The ability, or power, to exclude prevents the property from becoming common property, and the ability to alienate and to derive income permits the realization of gains from exchange.[1] Since restrictions generally reduce freedom of action, restrictions on a person's property rights reduce the value of the property to its owner. Thus it would appear that such restrictions are harmful.[2] In this section I will demonstrate that restrictions that seem to attenuate rights in fact often help to delineate rights more clearly.

Restrictions, that is, non-price allocations, can have no useful role in the Walrasian model. According to that model prices alone can direct all resources into their highest-value uses and will yield efficient allocation, since price adjustments are costless and rights are well defined. Restrictions, then, are at best superfluous and may well result in lower output. The unfavorable attitude by economists toward restrictions on, or attenuation of, rights may reflect the implicit application of the Walrasian, costless-transacting model.

In spite of the Walrasian model, restrictions on individuals' freedom to do what they wish with "their" property are widespread even in capital-

---

[1] The terms of alienation – whether price discrimination is legally permitted, whether sale is subject to price control, and how easily buyers can collude when dealing with the seller – affect the value of the rights.

[2] An owner is not harmed by a restriction if it existed before the property was acquired. The owner is harmed only if the restriction was imposed subsequent to purchase. The latter situation is likely to involve the use of resources to abet the harmful effects.

ist market economies. For instance, store owners are sometimes prohibited from opening at night or on Sundays, automobile operators are not allowed to transport paying passengers unless they acquire a "medallion," owners of water rights in the western United States are not free to sell the water to others or to divert it to new uses, and the size and location of structures that may be erected on urban lots are restricted by zoning regulations.

In these examples the government imposes the restrictions; but restrictions are not the exclusive domain of government. Some home owners are subject to private covenants – restrictions superimposed on those of governmental zoning. In addition, stockholders who own corporations are severely restricted as to what they may do with their properties, and fixed-rent tenants are often restricted with regard to the crops they may grow. These sets of private, voluntary restrictions were imposed by the original developers of such projects. Both the landowners who introduced the restrictions and the developers of the housing projects and of the corporations presumably believed that the restrictions would increase the net value of the projects to their buyers, thereby increasing the total net amount they themselves could extract. If this is so, the apparent inconsistency between wealth maximization and ownership restrictions must be just that – apparent and not real.

DIVIDED OWNERSHIP AND
RESTRICTIONS ON OWNERS

As I stated previously, commodities may be viewed as collections of many attributes whose levels tend to vary from one specimen of a commodity to another. Individuals sometimes choose to divide the ownership of commodity attributes among themselves because the most efficient owner of one attribute is not necessarily the most efficient owner of other attributes of the same commodity. When different attributes of a commodity are owned by different individuals, a special effort is required to exclude each of them from using attributes belonging to any of the others. One way to effect exclusion is to impose restrictions on the ways owners may exercise their rights such that the commodities will not become common property too easily. As viewed here, one function of restrictions on commodity ownership is to secure rights better by making exclusion easier to enforce. Such restrictions tend to prevent non-owners from consuming those attributes that belong to others. Restrictions on non-owners cannot be usefully viewed as attenuation.

The way a refrigerator is owned is a straightforward, convenient example of the role of divided ownership and of the corresponding restrictions. The sale of refrigerators to final consumers does not constitute an outright transfer, since the manufacturers retain responsibility for – that is, they remain the owners of – the attributes that are subject to warranty and those for which they are liable.[3] It is clear that manufacturers are more efficient owners than consumers of the potentially lethal leakage of the coolant, because it is their actions during the manufacturing process that largely determine whether or not the coolant will escape. Manufacturers are also the more efficient owners of the longevity of the motors. The longevity of motors depends, to a great extent, on manufacturing procedures about which manufacturers are informed at a low cost and consumers are uninformed. Refrigerator buyers, then, become the owners of only a subset of refrigerators' attributes. Given that the motor is subject to a warranty, they do not bear the entire cost of the motors' short lives; given liability, they do not acquire ownership of attributes such as "leakage of coolant." The advantage of divided ownership becomes evident when alienation is desirable. This is the case not only when a new refrigerator is transferred from manufacturer to wholesaler to retailer and ultimately to consumer; it is also desirable when a used refrigerator is offered for sale.

Consumers who decide to sell their refrigerators will transfer to buyers only those attributes that they own. If they were the owners of the attribute "leakage of coolant," they would encounter difficulties in arranging a sale contract, since they would be able to provide satisfactory information about that attribute only at a high cost to themselves. The manufacturers, on the other hand, who are the efficient owners of "leakage of coolant," remain liable for it; they continue to own this attribute. The refrigerator owners, therefore, are not involved with the transfer of the "leakage of coolant" attribute, and the sale of those remaining refrigerator attributes that are easier to alienate is correspondingly facilitated.

When ownership of a commodity – a physical entity – is divided, the owners of some attributes may have easy access to those that are owned by the others and may be able to treat them as free. For instance, buyers of a guaranteed product are likely to be less careful with it than they would be were it not warranteed; to them, the service covered by the warranty becomes a free attribute. In Chapter 3, in the course of a discussion of the tenancy contract, I showed how restrictions can reduce the cost associated with free attributes. Restrictions seem to play a similar role here. For instance, refrigerator manufacturers retain ownership of liabil-

[3] The manufacturers retain ownership of income streams that have only zero or negative values. They are the residual claimants, i.e., responsible for *those negative income streams*. Payments to the manufacturers for these potential services come ahead of time, when the original transactions are concluded.

ity and warranty attributes only if consumers submit to restrictions on such things as abuse and commercial use. Such restrictions help to isolate the attributes owned by the manufacturers from encroachment by consumers, thereby lowering dissipation, or capture, costs. The ownership of refrigerators by consumers is attenuated by such restrictions: Those who use their refrigerators commercially stand to lose the warranty protection. When a warranty is voided because the warranteed product is being used commercially, a consumer is being penalized for failing to heed a restriction. Not attenuated, for example, is the consumer's ownership of the right to decide what foods to store in the refrigerator; he or she owns this particular attribute. Indeed, because the restriction on commercial use reduces capture costs, it increases the net value of the original transaction; in other words, it increases the value of the remaining attributes.

Restrictions must be enforced in order to be effective; such enforcement is costly, but not uniformly so. For instance, commercial use of refrigerators can be easily proved; therefore, manufacturers make the warranty conditional on private use. Plain carelessness is too expensive to police, and careless behavior is not restrained. Conversely, the duration of the warranty is shortened when careless behavior is expensive to police – paint on refrigerators is guaranteed for a much shorter time than are motors.

The value of a transaction is another factor that helps to determine whether constraints will accompany it. In low-value transactions, the cost of managing restrictions can easily exceed the associated gains. Normally, as the value of transactions increases, more restrictions will be imposed and more resources will be devoted to their enforcement. Not surprisingly, both the manufacture and the use of commercial airplanes are associated with more restrictions than are the use and manufacture of automobiles. As a rule, airlines contract for the manufacture of specifically designated airplanes and monitor the performance of the manufacturer by stationing their own engineers on site. Airplane manufacturers, in turn, keep track of the airplanes they have produced after they are delivered to airlines.

RESTRICTIONS AND THE COST OF POLICE PROTECTION

Restrictions on ownership may perform another function, related to the protection of assets against theft. Because assets are always in danger of being stolen, ownership is never entirely secure. Theft can take many forms, and protection is also multidimensional. The state, through the police and the courts, provides protection against theft. The state, however, is not necessarily the most efficient protector against all aspects of theft. For instance, car owners can protect their cars cheaply by parking in well-lighted areas and by not leaving their engine running. They can also buy private protection in the market by installing theft-deterrence devices in their cars and by parking in lots with attendants.

Two features of the state's provision of policing services bear on the question of how to lower the resource cost of protection. First, the state commits itself to assist in the protection of legally delineated properties against theft. Second, police services are supplied at no marginal charge to individuals. Individuals may attempt to reduce their own efforts at protection and rely primarily on the police even where the returns on their activities do not justify the associated costs of policing, or where they can provide protection less expensively than the police. The state can reduce such excessive use of police services by imposing certain restrictions on individuals. Accordingly, the state stipulates that automobiles must be equipped with locks and that individuals must lock their cars when they leave them.[4]

In light of the preceding discussion, the next three sections are devoted to the interpretation of three sets of restrictive practices. The first section deals with restrictions imposed by the government on water ownership in the western United States;[5] next I explore government restrictions on homesteaders; and finally I discuss private restrictions imposed on two firms, one of which turns Chrysler hardtops into convertibles, and the other of which engages in the long-term storage of a truck manufacturer's replacement parts.

RESTRICTIONS ON WESTERN WATER OWNERS

Two distinct legal doctrines govern the use of water in the United States. In the eastern states, the prevailing system, originating in English common law, is riparian, permitting landowners reasonable use of water from rivers that run by their properties. Water is relatively abundant in that region (as it is in England), and so naturally the rights to it are rather loosely defined.[6] In contrast, many of the western states are arid, and the prevailing system is appropriative, granting individuals more complete

---

[4] Lueck (1989) suggests that the state restriction on trade in game-animal products may be explained by the attempt to reduce poaching.

[5] This section relies heavily on Miller (1985).

[6] Rose (1990) analyzes changes within the riparian system brought about primarily by the emergence of large-scale use of water for power for which previous rights were not well defined.

rights to water.[7] The flow of water in western streams varies significantly both seasonally and annually. Priorities concerning the water in these streams are relatively clearly defined.[8] The more thorough delineation of rights to water in the West is consistent with its aridity and with the correspondingly higher value of water there. The rights individuals have over "their" water are severely restricted. The balance of this section concerns the function of the restrictions on water ownership in the West.

The most severe restrictions on owners of rights to water in the western states regulate how the water is to be used. Most western states prohibit owners from using water for any purpose other than the one it originally served; the owners of rights to water are not allowed to sell them unless the sale includes the land where the water is used, and they are not even free to use the water on their own properties in any way they wish.

Like other commodities, the commodity "water" is composed of many attributes. Recognition of that fact is crucial if one is to understand why the delineation of rights to water is costly, why owners of water are not allowed to do whatever they wish with it in order to maximize its net value, and why owners' rights are attenuated. A special characteristic of water is that its abundance (and quality) downstream vary according to how individuals upstream use it. Whether or not the individual receives water depends, in part, on how much of the water that individuals with greater seniority have the right to divert seeps back into the stream – in other words, on what portion of the water withdrawn by those with higher priorities is returned to the stream. One person's realized right to water depends on the mode others take in exercising their own rights.

Were measurement costless, individuals would presumably be granted rights to remove a certain *net* amount of water from a stream. A person with a right to a net amount of 100 acre-feet of water could, for instance, withdraw 250 acre-feet to irrigate a crop if it was clear that 150 acre-feet would seep back into the stream. Measurement, however, is not costless; it is much cheaper to measure the amount of water removed from a stream than it is to measure the amount returned to it by seepage. Similar considerations apply to other attributes of water. It is easier to measure attributes such as salinity and temperature for the water withdrawn from

[7] Anderson and Hill (1975), among the first to systematize the analysis of property rights, offer an embryonic explanation of the transition from riparian to appropriative rights to water in the western states.

[8] The priorities reflect the initial order of the individual claims on water in the streams. The amount of water originally granted to individuals was in accord with the amount actually used in their operations, usually farming. As is pointed out in the next section, individuals' participation in rights protection seems easier when one owns just what one uses.

a river than it is to measure the same attributes for the water in the return flow.[9]

The original owners of water rights to a given stream presumably used the water for a specific purpose, for example, to irrigate an orchard. The precise contents of the grant of a low-priority right is a function of what the higher-priority holders are allowed to do. People with rights to withdraw water from a stream who are restricted to a specific use have rights that are delineated more narrowly, and are consequently less valuable, than they would be in the absence of the restriction. As a result of the restriction, however, the rights of those people with lower priorities and the rights to the two groups combined are more clearly delineated. In other words, whereas the rights of people with high priorities are attenuated, the rights of those with lower priorities are thereby enhanced. The more clearly rights in general are delineated, the more they are valued, since less is expected to be spent on their capture.

Two observed practices lend support to the hypothesis that the state-imposed restriction on water use is intended to increase the value of water rights. The first regards the inter-organization transfer of water. Mutual ditch companies and irrigation districts are permitted to use water in a way that seems to evade the regulation of water transfer. These organizations of neighbors are permitted to combine the water rights of their members. The restriction on transfers within each organization is avoided, enabling members to improve the allocation of water among themselves. Provided that the pattern of water use is not altered, the return quantity (and quality) of the water is likewise not altered. The greater flexibility available to these organizations, then, does not significantly impinge on the rights of others. Allowing water transfer within ditch companies and within irrigation districts is therefore consistent with the explanation that the purpose of the more general constraint on transfers is to enhance the clear delineation of rights.

The second practice concerns the distinct form of the constraint on water use that is applied in New Mexico. In that state water rights are defined in terms of consumption, that is, the net amount of water retained by the owner. Among the western states, New Mexico is one of the most arid, and it consequently values its water highly; so it is not surprising that it finds the costs of the added measurement that consump-

---

[9] Because it is easier to measure the volume of water than it is to measure some of its other attributes, it is relatively easy to see that a reduction by one owner of the amount of water returned to the stream will not reduce the amount of water available to higher-priority owners even if they are located farther downstream than the lower-priority users. But a reduction in the quality of returned water will tend to reduce the water quality available to all those downstream, regardless of their priority. This implies that, priorities remaining constant, the value of the right to water in a given stream is likely to decline the farther downstream it is.

tion rights entail to be worthwhile. The relative ease with which owners
of water rights in New Mexico may obtain the regulator's permission to
sell water is consistent with the interpretation that constraints play a role
in better delineating rights.[10]

HOMESTEADING

Before 1776, all land in the colonial United States had been initially de-
clared to be the property of the British crown. British authorities employed various methods of dispensing land, including granting it to
states, trading companies, and individuals who crossed the Atlantic. The
transfer of power in 1776 was accompanied by a change in the land-
release policy. The federal government of the United States adopted a
more unified policy of managing its land holdings, one element of which
was to discourage "preemption" – the priority right of the illegal settlers,
or squatters, to buy the land on which they had settled.

Until the Louisiana Purchase in 1803, most U.S. government–owned
land was in the thirteen original states, and market sales of government
land were routine. During the nineteenth century the U.S. government
took possession of vast amounts of land in the West. Abundant as the
land was, the government made a concerted effort to prevent its becoming common property. As the population grew, the government continued
to sell land in some areas. In others the government periodically released
for settlement blocks of land that were not handled in a conventional
commercial fashion. The government could have auctioned off these parcels of land or set a price, or a price structure, at which to sell whatever
acreage buyers wanted to purchase. Instead, passing various acts, the best
known of which is the Homestead Act of 1862, the government either
set a price substantially below the market price or charged no price at
all. At the same time it imposed severe constraints that those claiming
land had to satisfy before they could gain the right to sell the land.

A possible explanation for these government restrictions is that they
were imposed in order to induce settlers' self-protection against raids
where such protection was cheaper than direct protection by the state.
Had all unsettled land been placed in the public domain or made available for sale, so that anyone could have settled in any unoccupied area,
the cost to the state of protecting settlers would have been high. Such
costs, particularly in isolated or hostile areas, could have exceeded the
net value of the newly settled areas to their owners. On the other hand,

[10]Johnson, Gisser, and Werner (1981) discuss water rights in New Mexico in a
similar vein. In a study of water rights in four western states, Gisser (1995) elaborates
on the analysis I offer here. He demonstrates a strong trend toward a clearer delineation of rights to water in New Mexico and a fitful trend in Arizona, California, and
Texas.

the total cost of protecting an area and the share of the government in such cost declined as the density of settlers in the area increased. Similarly, these costs declined if the new area abutted previously settled areas.

Whereas the government routinely seemed to take upon itself the protection of its people and their property, the government as the *owner* of the land could relatively easily withhold protection from areas it chose to keep unoccupied. By categorizing whoever was occupying empty land as an interloper or a squatter, the government reduced its obligation to protect such people. Because the government was the owner of the land, the decision as to whether an area was valuable enough to justify its settlement rested with itself. It could take into account the cost of protection in determining whether to open a new area for settlement.

The restrictions associated with homesteading, particularly those imposed by the 1862 act, are consistent with the hypothesis that their function was to induce self-protection. Dense settlement enhances self-protection and economizes on policing and military costs in general.[11] Correspondingly, homesteading was practiced in areas where Indian nations were most likely to contest settlement by whites, not in areas where such a threat was absent. A central feature of homesteading was for the government to select a unit of land large enough (160 acres) to support a family and to restrict each settler to one such unit.[12] A less obvious but equally important feature was the attempt to ensure that the land would actually be densely occupied. This may help explain not only the low pecuniary price (zero in 1862) of the land[13] but also the federal government's policy of waiting to open new land for homesteading until the land became so valuable that a large fraction of the units open for homesteading had a good chance of being claimed.[14] This underpricing policy is probably what generated the excitement associated with the opening of new lands.[15] Homesteaders had to satisfy two additional constraints

[11] In the first edition of this book I considered only self-protection. The more general hypothesis is due to Allen (1991).

[12] In later acts applying to the more arid land farther west, the unit was increased to up to 640 acres.

[13] Settlers, however, could preempt the land for $1.25 per acre after six months' residence.

[14] This argument parallels Cheung's (1977) regarding the phenomenon of owners "underpricing" the better movie theater seats in order to get those seats fully (or densely) occupied, thereby securing effective policing by the patrons themselves.

[15] All homesteads in each newly opened area were released by the government under the same set of constraints even though they were not all equally valued. Allocation of individual homesteads was on a first-come, first-served basis, allowing the earliest arriver to claim the best homestead. In order to get a head start, some jumped the gun; hence the term "Sooner." Conversely, the lowest-value homesteads remained unclaimed. The Graduation Act of 1854 provided for progressive price reductions for such unclaimed land.

before they were granted full ownership of the land: (1) They actually had to occupy the homestead for at least five years, and (2) they had to improve the land before acquiring the right to sell it. These two restrictions are consistent with the objective of dense settlement: They make leaving costly. The limited duration of these requirements presumably reflects the desire of the government to enhance efficient cultivation – to permit the exchange of land in order to reach holdings of an efficient farm size[16] and an efficient level of labor input.[17]

Texas is unique among the states in that it joined the union as a republic, not a territory, and the public land there was held by the state rather than the federal government. Although it faced serious protection problems, after it joined the union the cost of protection was borne by the union as a whole. Prior to joining the union, the state subsidized and restricted new border settlers. That the purpose of the policy was to enhance protection is demonstrated by the fact that after joining the union, the state made virtually no land grants to settlers, instead selling land in order to release it.[18]

PRIVATE CONSTRAINTS, MAXIMIZATION, AND VERTICAL INTEGRATION

Making convertibles for Chrysler

In the two previous sections I have attempted to explain the role of governmental constraints on private ownership. The constraints discussed in this section[19] are strictly those between private parties. In 1984 – and most likely in other years as well – Chrysler contracted with another firm (seemingly Cars and Concepts, Inc.) to turn its automobiles into convertibles. That firm did not act as a subcontractor; it *purchased* the auto bodies from Chrysler and then performed the conversion. By purchasing the auto bodies, the conversion firm presumably became the owner of these automobiles; nevertheless, its ownership was severely constrained. First, the contract between the two firms stipulated that only Chrysler could purchase the converted cars. Second, the repurchase terms

---

[16] The size of the individual holding and the consolidation of holdings presented particularly acute problems where the land was used for grazing, which requires large blocks of land.

[17] Allen (1991) elaborates on the hypothesis that the purpose of the Homestead Act was to reduce the cost of protection by government. He ingeniously exploits differences in conditions across the United States (and other countries) and the changes from the 1860s to the 1930s to test the hypothesis, which his results conclusively support.

[18] The Texas account is taken from Allen 1991.

[19] The information in this section was provided through casual conversation.

123

were stipulated ahead of time; Chrysler agreed to buy only cars whose conversions met its specifications and at a predetermined price. Finally, the conversion firm guaranteed the conversion; when selling the convertibles to the public, Chrysler guaranteed them but turned guarantee work concerning the conversion over to the conversion firm. It may appear, then, that the rights of the conversion firm were attenuated. Upon further examination, however, it becomes clear that the restrictions effectively delineated ownership.

Of course, Chrysler could have operated very differently. It could have created a separate department or division to make convertibles. In that case, however, the head of that department would necessarily have been a Chrysler *employee*. Since employees' pay is not strictly a function of performance, the incentive of the manager to economize would not have been as strong as that of the residual claimant to the conversion operation. Inducements such as bonuses and stock options would have helped but could not have resolved the problem fully.

The constraints Chrysler imposed on the conversion firm provided the latter with a strong incentive to perform the conversion efficiently without impinging on Chrysler's own profits. It would have retained any cost reduction it was able to effect and would have lost the value of cars that could not meet the repurchase specifications. The critical success of such vertical disintegration must have hinged crucially on the transactors' ability to cheaply measure the conversion-related attributes of both the cars Chrysler first sold and those it later repurchased.[20] The relative ease of measurement of these attributes permitted the conversion firm to become, in effect, the owner not of whole cars but of the conversion attributes of these cars. Far from attenuating the rights of the conversion firm, the restrictions permitted that firm to become the owner of a subset of attributes and then to assume the consequences of its own operations, thereby largely removing its incentive to shirk.

Storing truck parts

For several years Sajac, a firm specializing in long-term storage, stored spare parts made by Paccar for the Kenworth and Peterbilt trucks Paccar manufactured. The contract between Paccar and Sajac stipulated, among other things:

[20] According to Williamson's (1975) and Klein, Crawford, and Alchian's (1978) view, it may seem that the conversion firm was earning quasi-rents capturable by Chrysler. If measurement of the pertinent magnitudes is indeed easy, then disputes can be decided in the courts relatively cheaply. The fundamental problem is not that of the capture of quasi-rents but, rather, that of the measurability of the attributes of the transaction, which in this case did not pose a serious problem.

1. Sajac would pay Paccar the scrap price for the parts.
2. For a four-year period after receiving a batch of parts, Sajac would make the parts available only to Paccar.
3. Beyond the four-year-period, Sajac would have the option of scrapping the parts or continuing to store them and to make them available to Paccar.
4. For parts Paccar ordered back from Sajac, Paccar would pay 90 percent of the accounting cost.
5. Paccar could refuse to accept parts it determined not to be in good condition.

This arrangement was advantageous to Paccar for income-tax purposes, since the Internal Revenue Service (IRS) had stipulated a few years earlier that firms such as Paccar could not write off the cost of parts they did not actually sell. By selling the parts to Sajac at just a fraction of the accounting cost of these parts, Paccar was able to write these parts off. The IRS, however, challenged Paccar's write-off of the parts transferred to Sajac, claiming that the transaction did not constitute a sale because a sale requires a change of ownership, and conditions such as items 2–5 in the list ensured that Paccar would remain the true owner of the parts. Granted that the tax incentive induced the arrangement at least in part, what accounts for its odd features?

The view that commodities are made up of many attributes and that it is sometimes advantageous not to have a single person or a single firm own all of them suggests that there is no definitive answer to the IRS challenge.[21] Paccar did remain the owner of some attributes of the parts, but Sajac became the owner of others, namely, the storage attributes. Sajac's gains came primarily from lowering the costs of storage and from selling the parts back to Paccar. Sajac apparently made efforts in both respects: It maintained facilities for low-cost, long-term storage, and it devoted resources – essentially making sales pitches – to bring to the attention of Paccar's replacement-parts division the availability of various parts it was storing even though it appeared that Paccar continued to own the parts.

It seems that Paccar's main objectives in restricting Sajac to selling the parts back were to maintain its own reputation and to prevent Sajac from taking a ride on the Paccar brand name by selling truck drivers low-quality parts bearing Paccar's name. Paccar could have protected its brand name by storing the parts directly or by renting space from Sajac in which to store the parts, thereby retaining control of their quality. In neither case would the incentives for efficient storage have been as strong

---

[21] The court, however, ruled for the IRS.

as they were in the actual case, where the reward, on the margin, belonged entirely to the firm in charge of the storage.

Vertical relationships

The relationships between Paccar and the storage firm and between Chrysler and the conversion firm shed light on the problem of vertical integration. Like other firms, both Paccar and Chrysler are only partially vertically integrated. In our daily lives we are so used to observing highly integrated firms[22] that we fail to ask why every individual does not operate as an "independent" one-person firm. The preceding discussion of the relationship between the two pairs of firms points to some of the gains resulting from operating independently. When people assume ownership, they also assume responsibility for their own behavior. On the other hand, when people work as others' employees, or when other production factors are rented out, shirking is to be expected. When two independent firms perform operations that would otherwise have been performed within a single firm, however, a market exchange is required. As I previously argued, any exchange consumes resources, and effecting full alienation is often expensive. Correspondingly, most exchanges involve only subsets of the attributes of the goods involved. In the case of the truck-parts storage, Sajac, which bought the parts, seems to have operated independently of Paccar, but its operations were severely constrained. Nevertheless, these operations were much less constrained than they would have been had they been carried out within Paccar. Sajac was more of a residual claimant to the storage operations than a Paccar division would have been. Presumably the costs of the partial alienation of the parts – first from Paccar and then back to it – were relatively low; therefore Sajac, the storage firm, assumed responsibility for the storage operation. The costliness of transferring other spare-parts attributes seems to be the reason Paccar restricted Sajac to return of the parts rather than allowing it to dispense them without constraint.[23]

CONCLUSION

The costliness of transacting makes undesirable side effects a virtually inevitable consequence of exchange. Ownership of commodities by more

[22] A supermarket, for instance, is a firm that sells a huge array of products and whose employees perform a wide variety of vertical (as well as horizontal) operations.
[23] The ambiguity regarding who the true owner of the parts was, and consequently the nature of Paccar's scope of operations, illustrates Cheung's (1983) observation concerning the difficulty of determining what a firm actually is, and points to the advantage of concentrating on contracts.

than one person is a major source of side effects because the owner of a subset of a commodity's attributes can relatively easily consume without charge some of the attributes belonging to others. It is too expensive, however, to price and police all the effects associated with transactions. One method of reducing the costs of the attempted capture by some people of others' rights is to impose constraints on the former. One farmer might be able to capture another farmer's water by switching to a crop that returns less of the withdrawn water to the stream. The latter's rights can be protected, however, by not allowing the former to use water to irrigate new crops. Such restrictions serve to make rights clearer, thereby enhancing them even though they may superficially appear to attenuate them.

As the costs associated with a restriction rise, new methods of protecting rights are expected to emerge. When the value of a new crop or of the water itself increases, I expect that protection of the rights of lower-priority owners of water rights will be enhanced through the use of a more expensive and more accurate method of measuring the water used by high-priority owners. The more accurate metering of the actual use of the water itself should permit the relaxation of indirect constraints on the use of water, such as the choice of which crops to grow, and the granting to owners of water rights greater freedom in trading those rights.

The restrictions on water use and the restrictions on homesteaders have been government-imposed. The framework in which they were discussed is the same as the framework for the private restrictions Chrysler and Paccar imposed on their exchange partners. In each of these cases I assume that every decision is ultimately made by maximizing individuals. In none of the cases are marginal costs expected to be equated with the corresponding marginal valuations. In each case, however, forces inclining toward such equalization are assumed to be present. This point will be elaborated on briefly in the next chapter.

9

Property rights and non-market allocation

The property rights approach to the study of economics has been promoted by market-oriented economists, who have used it occasionally to demonstrate the superiority of the market. Contrary to the perception that property rights tools may best be used to analyze the market economy, where allocation is performed largely if not entirely by prices, these tools seem to be uniquely well suited to analyzing resource allocation in non-market settings. Under the Walrasian approach, where rights are perfectly defined, nothing is lost by quickly dispensing with the topic of property rights, for there is little to say about them within that model, where prices determine everything. Indeed, the Walrasian model may provide satisfactory answers to many problems in capitalist economies, where prices play a vital role in economic life.

Those economists who have contributed most to the study of property rights tend to be strong advocates of unregulated markets. They contend that people and the economy thrive when left to their own devices, and that government intervention tends to reduce wealth. In the market, the argument goes, prices move resources to their highest-value uses; when prices are not given the opportunity to perform their function, misallocation results. Government intervention is deemed acceptable in such areas as national defense, police, the courts, and the money supply; such intervention is said to be desirable only inasmuch as it facilitates the functioning of markets. Despite the prevalence of this reasoning, government regulations cannot be dismissed on a priori grounds. In this chapter, I explore some of the conditions under which government regulations may complement or enhance the actions of individuals.

For non-market economies, where market prices are eschewed or suppressed, the Walrasian model is incapable of explaining how resources are allocated. Here the property rights approach attains the utmost importance in the analysis of decisions about allocation. The irony is great, for champions of the free market have developed tools that are most

powerful when they are used to analyze non-market – including socialist – economies.[1] Although I believe that the property-rights approach
applies to all human behavior and to all human institutions, any serious
attempt to demonstrate this would prove too lengthy and too speculative.
In support of the assertion I shall, however, first offer a brief discussion
of the applicability of the property rights approach to two specific areas
of non-market allocation: (1) allocation by voting in market settings,
where it is shown that individuals sometimes choose to bypass the market
and instead adopt non-market allocation devices, and (2) allocation by
voluntary charitable behavior, where it clearly demonstrates an advantage over market behavior. I will then briefly examine the function of
private property rights and the method of inducing people to perform in
a non-market economy.

ALLOCATION BY VOTING

On occasion individuals allocate resources by voting – a mechanism that
explicitly bypasses the use of prices in favor of non-price allocation. Individuals who use markets retain control of how they use their wealth,
maintaining full discretion over what to purchase. Within voting organizations, on the other hand, individuals are subject to constraints imposed
on them by their fellow voters. Yet by their own behavior individuals
demonstrate that they value some of these constraints even though they
reduce their freedom of action.

Voting is used not only in the public sector but also in many profit-
seeking settings, including shareholder corporations (mostly to elect of-
ficers) and in condominiums (to make an array of operating decisions).
The origins of organizations such as corporations and condominiums, in
which voting is used, lie in the operations of entrepreneurs. In the case of
condominiums, for example, developers typically erect the housing units
and related structures and complete other preparatory work before selling the units to individual buyers. Developers do not have to sell housing
units as condominiums. Another option, one that maintains the owner-
occupier tax advantage, is to sell the units to individual buyers, who operate independently of one another. It is presumed that developers will
generally choose the method of sale that promises the largest difference
between the aggregate selling price of their units and the costs they incur.

In fact, condominium developers are offering buyers packages that
consist of both the physical structures and the rules that will govern some
aspects of the prospective owners' future behavior – rules that include

---

[1] As Wing Suen pointed out to me, the irony is compounded by the championing of
the use of prices in socialist systems by such eminent economists as Lerner and Lange.

decisions by voting. These developers offer the units as condominiums rather than independent ones because they expect their buyers to pay a higher price for condominiums than they would if they were to purchase the units independently. Clearly, condominium buyers value packages that *constrain* them to allocate resources by voting (e.g., on whether or not to build a swimming pool) *more* than they value deals that, by contrast, allow decisions regarding the supply of such services to be made in the market.

Although no attempt will be made here to explain the rationale for such behavior,[2] individuals reveal through their behavior that they sometimes prefer non-price allocation to allocation by price.[3] The use of prices, then, is not always the most efficient method of allocation. The next section points to one advantage of non-market allocation.

DONATED BLOOD VERSUS PURCHASED BLOOD

An attempt to demonstrate that unhindered markets are best is found in Kessel's (1974) analysis of blood donation. The puzzle he attempted to solve was why, when blood was purchased, the incidence of hepatitis among transfusion recipients was higher than when it was donated. Kessel examined both the mechanisms used to provide blood and the apparent advantage donated blood had over purchased blood in avoiding the transmission of hepatitis. He reached the conclusion that a more vigorous pursuit of profits would have secured higher-quality blood in the market. Despite his masterful command of theory and evidence, Kessel's explanation of why the market for blood did not function adequately and why, in fact, blood purchased in the market was no bargain is not compelling.

Missing from Kessel's model is the recognition that effecting market transactions is itself costly. Alternative mechanisms, where resources are allocated by inducements other than price, can sometimes generate a higher net gain than market transactions. The analysis of non-market organization for the supply of blood will provide a different explanation as to why the quality of donated blood is higher than that of purchased blood.

Blood, like other commodities, is a collection of attributes whose levels vary from one specimen to another. In particular, some blood specimens

[2] See Barzel and Sass 1990, for a detailed discussion of this topic.
[3] Developers who construct housing units in unincorporated areas, to be sold as condominiums and to be managed by a homeowners' association, are basically developing whole political units. In this case incorporation is an option for residents. Presumably developers take this into account. Here a political unit may emerge as a consequence of the quest for profit. Buyers implicitly choose the associated political restrictions.

are infected with hepatitis while others are free of it. The lower the probability that a batch of blood is infected with hepatitis, the more valuable it is. In general, buyers would not pay a high price for the low-quality specimen if they could costlessly (or at least cheaply) assess it, as the Walrasian model assumes, but this is not the case in the market for blood. By simply posting the two prices at which they would be willing to buy the two types of blood, buyers are unlikely to secure the desired qualities. Because sellers prefer selling their products at higher prices, blood buyers need to be able to determine which grade of blood they are getting if they wish to avoid paying the higher price for the inferior commodity. In the time period Kessel investigated, however, the test for hepatitis infection in blood was virtually worthless, so it was difficult for buyers to distinguish between the two kinds of blood. As a consequence, the market for blood performed poorly, and the proportion of infected specimens purchased was high.

Despite the inaccuracy of tests, knowledge of whether any blood specimen was or was not tainted with hepatitis was not always difficult to come by, because people often know – or at least suspect – when they are carriers of the disease. The problem is that impersonal markets are ill-suited for extracting the information and determining the quality of such a commodity as blood. Because information about blood is not costless to *all* concerned, the value of market exchanges of blood is greatly lowered. The information is free to a subset of individuals – the sellers – but the market is unlikely to extract the information costlessly because sellers, who can gain by concealing it, are able to do so.

Using a monetary reward happens to be disadvantageous for securing hepatitis-free blood. The incidence of hepatitis among drug addicts is high because they tend to infect one another by sharing needles; these are the same individuals for whom cash for blood is a particularly attractive trade.[4] The attempt to purchase blood in the open market, then, is likely to attract a relatively large proportion of carriers.[5] Separation is nevertheless possible, but not within the unrestricted market setting. Obtaining blood from donors instead of purchasing it for cash alters the selection criteria of suppliers because it tends to cheaply screen out people who know they are carriers. Would-be donors must be persuaded to donate. They respond because they wish to help other human beings. People who

---

[4] The fact that transacting is costly and needs facilitating suggests that cash is not as neutral as it is often thought to be. If, for example, blood sellers were paid in non-transferable tuition vouchers, it seems highly likely that the fraction of infected addicts among sellers would be smaller than it was with cash as the means of payment.

[5] Kessel identified various methods of screening out individuals who are likely to be carriers. These methods, however, are costly. Sellers of blood were generally not screened, which implies that the cost of screening must have been too high.

know or suspect that they are carriers are aware that their donation will do harm. They are simply expected not to donate.

Of course, cash markets are not used by accident; they economize on some of the costs of effecting exchange. The use of donors in lieu of cash markets incurs costs that are absent from cash markets. For instance, volunteers are not generally the lowest-cost suppliers of the commodity or service they donate. The costs and gains of using markets as compared with other allocation methods, such as charity, differ across commodities. Given the difficulty of testing for the presence of hepatitis and the HIV virus that causes AIDS, blood is one commodity for which the advantages of non-market over market allocation are evident.

The cash-market sellers' ability to gain by knowingly passing off low-quality specimens as high in quality is common to many commodities besides blood. Nevertheless, charity is not expected to be used in all such cases. The precise nature of the quality problem is likely to differ from one commodity to another, and each should generate its own charitable response. Mechanisms other than charity may be more effective in securing the desired quality for some of these commodities.

Although a donor's motive for choosing one charity over another seems to be a matter of taste, one simple prediction can be derived: It seems reasonable to assume that, like other actions, charitable giving will expand when the gains it generates become larger.[6] On the issue of blood, it is predicted that in the span of time after the discovery that blood could be infected with the HIV virus but before effective tests for it were devised, the amount of blood donated relative to that sold for cash increased substantially.

ALLOCATION BY GOVERNMENT

The government of every country plays an important role in economic activity, and some governments' roles are enormous. All governments engage in non-business activities, such as conducting foreign affairs and operating the courts, and virtually all also engage, to varying degrees, in more businesslike activities, often conducting operations that in some other countries are run privately, usually for profit. It is occasionally argued that governments should seek profits when they manage their enter-

[6] This account does not offer an explanation as to why people give to charity, and it does not attempt to predict when people would give more or less. It does, however, shed light on the social value of inducing such a mode of behavior. To make the notion of giving operational, it is enough to assume that charity is a commodity that provides utility to some individuals, and then to apply to it the law of demand: The lower its unit cost, or the higher the unit benefit, the more units will be "consumed."

prises, and some government enterprises may actually seem to operate in that way. Even when profit maximization is the stated objective of the government enterprise, however, the identity of the residual claimants remains unclear.

The difficulty of identifying such individuals and the common claim that government is generally wasteful and inefficient both suggest to many that private-property rights are absent from government operations. Indeed, former communist countries claim to have abolished private-property rights, at least with regard to the means of production. I shall argue that private property rights must exist in a functioning economy.[7] I shall also argue that the notion that government is inefficient cannot be correct. After some general comments on individual maximization, I shall try to determine what can be inferred from the sheer existence of a government-run enterprise, using a city bus system as the example. I shall then consider the meaning of an arbitrary detail of its operations – the activities of bus drivers – and move on to more general aspects of the operation of such a system. I shall not inquire directly into what the proper areas for government activity are; rather, I am using a property-rights approach to offer a glimpse into the way a government functions.

The assumption of individual maximization is heavily exploited in economics literature that features an analysis of profit-seeking enterprises and private consumption. I wish to examine the implications of individual maximization for government operations. Because governments are run by people, government activity ultimately results from the interactions of maximizing individuals. Contrary to the implied assertion by some economists and other scholars, one consequence of maximizing behavior is that government actions are never deliberately wasteful or capricious. If "waste" means that some individuals lose from an action from which *no one* else gains, such an occurrence is inconsistent with maximizing. Whoever takes any kind of action must expect to gain from it; indeed, the perceived net gain must always be the largest one available.

An action that appears to others to have been wasteful must, nevertheless, have been expected to generate a gain to the person who undertook it. Moreover, such a person must not have believed he or she could gain more by acting differently. The resources under consideration are ultimately allocated to a particular use by whoever is in control of them. The logic behind the allocation is straightforward. Such resources have alternative uses, each with its own valuation. The ability of potential

[7] In the aftermath of the breakdown of Eastern European communism, many of the functionaries of these regimes who continued to operate in their old institutions actually landed on their feet. This implies that these individuals had substantial economic rights.

users to bid for the resources, however, is subject to constraints. For example, the constraints may be that bids may be made only by citizens or by party members. Similarly, bids may be restricted in form (e.g., lecture fees or promises of future high-paying jobs, open cash bids being prohibited).[8] Whatever the rationale for the constraints,[8] a maximizing controller of resources will allocate such resources to the person who makes the highest bid as determined by the controller. The winning bid generally is not the same as the one with the highest value in the absence of the constraints. In this regard, resources may appear to be wasted, particularly in the eyes of those who are not aware of the constraints. Given the constraints, however, other potential users of the resources that appear to have been wasted must not have bid high enough for them. Applying this reasoning somewhat more generally, it can be concluded that the lower the perceived net gain from an action to the individuals who have the right over it, the lower the chance that such an action will be taken, no matter how beneficial the action is supposed to be or how large its expected gains absent the constraints.[9] One must bear in mind that the higher the potential benefits of an action, the more the beneficiaries are able to bid for it; "ability," however, may be difficult to translate into an actual bid.

In order to be able to analyze individual behavior in a government organization, it is necessary to address the relationship between private ownership and government activity. Because maximizing people will act only when they expect to gain from their actions, one must be able to determine who gains and who loses from government actions in order to connect the actions with ownership. Selecting, for example, a city bus system, one must ask who owns it, that is, who has at least some of the power to consume its services, to obtain income from it, or to alienate its assets. The "city" is not a satisfactory answer, because it does not identify the individuals who gain when the buses are running on time and lose when they are not. Answering "the city" denies that such individuals exist and therefore implies the claim that there is no residual claimant to the operation of the bus system. Yet if no one gains from improving the operations of the bus system and no one loses by letting the system deteriorate, it must lie in the public domain. Allowing the bus system to deteriorate requires less effort than maintaining it, so it would cease to function if it lay in the public domain. Similarly, it cannot be true that the bus system lies in the public domain when access to its assets is constrained. For instance, in a functioning system, attempts to commandeer buses are

---

[8] The constraints are, of course, also imposed by individuals who are maximizing.
[9] The same considerations apply to the process of selecting government bureaucrats and government projects – and ultimately to the selection of the government itself.

likely to be punished. So long as the city bus system is not totally paralyzed, property rights over it must exist.[10] Various observed bus-system activities, which I outline in the following paragraphs, imply the specific existence of certain private property rights.

The fact that riders use city buses is an indication of the existence of a whole system of private rights. The activities of employed bus drivers illustrate the mechanics of this system. Employed drivers will be fired unless they perform some minimal level of services. The drivers engage in an exchange with their supervisors, and exchanges constitute a *reassignment* of property rights. Here the drivers acquire the right to a wage, while relinquishing some rights over themselves by performing driving services.

Drivers may be asked to do more than the specified minimum; if they are to perform beyond the minimum, they must be given an incentive. Such an incentive need not be higher pecuniary pay; it may take the form of a better chance for promotion, a more convenient work schedule, or an easier route. Whatever its form, no extra effort will be forthcoming without it. Drivers have at least some rights over themselves; they control, that is, they own the rights to, the level of effort, and they exchange rights over particular effort levels for other rights.

Employed drivers cannot operate in isolation. Someone in the bus system must gain from forming the contracts that induce the drivers to perform busing services. Similarly, the mere fact that drivers are given routes to drive and schedules to maintain implies that someone has been induced to perform the functions of creating the routes and schedules. It can likewise be inferred that certain individuals are induced to maintain buses; otherwise the buses would not be in operating condition. As long as bus lines operate, then, a whole array of people must be rewarded for performing individual functions. The bus system may be managed bureaucratically and may function sluggishly. Still, some property rights must be granted to the individuals associated with it; otherwise no service whatsoever would be forthcoming.

Governments often seem to set output targets at levels such that at the margin valuations differ from costs. In communist countries such goals were often stated explicitly. The constant shortages characteristic of such regimes arose from prices that had been set lower than was required to

[10] The claim, made by leaders of communist states, that private property there had been abolished and that all property belonged to the state seems to have been an attempt to divert attention from who the true owners of the property were. Evidently these owners also owned the rights to the terminology. It is ironic, at least in terms of the rhetoric, that communist states had a hard time keeping resources such as air and rivers from getting into the public domain (the ultimate in collective ownership!). As a result, the value of these resources was reduced to a level much lower than the one they occupy in capitalist states.

clear the market and from allocations that simply seemed arbitrary. Government enterprises were affected by such policies in various ways. How would the operations of the bus-system repair shop have been run under such conditions? Presumably, from time to time the repair shop would have been hampered by a shortage of parts. As long as buses were running, we must conclude that individuals in the repair shop were being rewarded for getting the buses to work and that the rewards were larger when the repair-shop services were better. Repair-shop personnel would have gained by having parts on hand, and consequently should have been willing to spend resources in order to secure them. They might, for instance, have attempted to trade with the repair shop of another city's bus system or with a truck repair shop. Alternatively, they might have offered a special reward to the parts producers for furnishing extra parts. Such producers, as is generally true under price controls, would not have been likely to produce at full potential for the controlled-price segment of the market. They might readily have been induced to expand output, however, if the reward had exceeded the control price.[11]

The details of such operations cannot be determined by an armchair economist, but maximizing behavior implies that the discrepancies between marginal valuation and marginal costs must generate forces toward their elimination. Indeed, as was shown in the discussion of price controls in Chapter 2, once the added adjustment of transaction costs is accounted for, the discrepancies must be eliminated entirely. This attainment of equilibrium simply follows from maximization. The equilibrium itself, however, is likely to differ from equilibria reached under different sets of constraints. Given the government-imposed restrictions, the adjustment costs may be so high that the final output may lag drastically behind the corresponding market outcome.

The advantages of allowing residual claimants to operate in an economy are clear. In the context of new opportunities for the bus system, suppose it is discovered that the residents of a new suburb are willing to pay more for bus service than this service would cost. If an individual were in charge of deciding whether or not to start service, and if he or she were also the sole claimant to the residual, service would be provided

---

[11] Some non-market economies are called "command" economies; a command economy is one in which the planner imposes an output target along with the control price. Imposing as the term may sound, it will be obeyed only if it sets low targets. Because inputs are never uniform, and because of random fluctuations, the output target the commander will set must, as a rule, fall short of maximum output. Otherwise, as in the case of slavery, the commander will incur losses by punishing those unable to obey the command because it is excessive. If output is costly to measure, shirking with regard to the target output may also occur. The quantity supplied, then, is expected to increase if the *reward* is larger; an increase will not be forthcoming if it is simply *commanded*.

because the individual would reap the difference between the gains and the cost. Moreover, such a service would be expanded until, on the margin, the cost equaled the gain.

In a political system, given the way such systems usually operate, the effect of demand forces is less direct, but it is definitely not absent. The system of rewards in government seldom compensates individuals for the full private gains they generate. An operator in the political realm unable to claim 100 percent of the residual would stop short of the level of service a private operator would reach. Although the same forces that bridge gaps created by price controls tend to prevent gaps between marginal valuations and marginal costs from growing ever larger, a full-fledged residual claimant is less handicapped than one who has only a partial claim; the full-fledged claimant will consequently produce what appears to be a more efficient outcome.

Why would an operator not be allowed to claim 100 percent of the residual? More generally, why are individuals not always allowed free rein to become residual claimants? Prohibitions must perform real functions. The superior who has constrained the operator presumably has the power to impose constraints.[12] Returning to the example of suburban bus service: The superior may have had no interest in increasing the operator's wealth but could still have been able to increase his or her own wealth by selling the right to serve the suburb. In order to answer the question regarding the absence of a full-fledged residual claimant, one must also ask what prevented the superior from selling the right to the operator or, even better, to the highest bidder. I conjecture that the answer lies in the fact that the seller's wealth depends not only on the pecuniary price but also on features of the buyer and of the exchanged property.

In general, maximizers may choose not to sell an asset or a franchise to the highest bidder. There are many reasons for this reluctance, all of which may be viewed as resulting from the presence of side effects. For instance, manufacturers sometimes pay their salespeople a commission or a salary instead of selling them the merchandise outright. By not granting salespeople full residual-claimant status, manufacturers ensure that their incentive for capturing wealth from other salespeople is tempered. In another case, persons who cannot fully guarantee their actions may be inclined to take unduly large risks. The incentive to undertake excessively risky projects where some of the risk is borne by third parties is reduced if the decision makers are not allowed to become full-fledged residual claimants.

One reason residual-claimant rights are not granted may apply primar-

---

[12] For simplicity, the superior here is assumed to possess the ultimate authority; people intermediate in the hierarchy are ignored.

ily to despotic regimes. The explanation has to do with the concentration of wealth that free enterprise entails. Bad luck may cause the holders of residual claims to experience financial ruin, whereas good fortune can render them rich. When many opportunities to assume residual claims are made available, at least a few individuals are likely to become rich. Rich people, particularly those whose wealth is not easy for others to keep track of, are in a position to finance coups. Such people pose a threat to the despot. This, I suspect, is one reason why dictators are often averse to free enterprise. Communist regimes' harsh treatment of "profiteers" may be a case in point. The suppression of opportunities that may enrich some individuals is costly to dictators, who could instead allow their exploitation while collecting a commensurate franchise fee. It is not that dictators are not assumed to be maximizers. Their longevity and the security of their status are what is viewed as valuable to them. They are willing to sacrifice pecuniary gains they could otherwise obtain by auctioning off various residual rights, because these would have posed a risk to their security. Instead, they prefer to operate bureaucratically – a less lucrative option but one that promises greater longevity.

CONCLUSION

The distinction between the private and public sectors is not to be equated with that between the presence and absence of private property rights. Such rights are necessarily present in both systems. The distinction lies instead in organization, particularly in the incentives and rewards under which producers tend to operate. In the private sector, producers have the opportunity to assume the entire direct effect of their actions. In the government sector, people assume a smaller portion of the direct effect of their actions. Both systems reflect the outcome of the actions of maximizers, and both must operate efficiently.

IO

Additional property rights applications

In previous chapters I demonstrated the expediency of using the property rights approach to explain various aspects of such specific phenomena as gasoline price controls and slavery, and to develop a general approach to, among other things, non-market allocation, the maximizing role of restrictions on private property rights, and, in the context of farm tenancy, the choice among various forms of control. The property rights framework can be applied to other problems as well. I shall now briefly consider several of these problems, beginning with an analysis of the individuals' ability to protect themselves against losses to monopoly, proceeding to a discussion of the relationship between property rights and theft and of property rights in relation to innovation and to price information, and concluding with an exploration of property rights as they relate to wildlife.

PROTECTION AGAINST LOSSES TO MONOPOLY

Monopolies are said to result in resource misallocation,[1] which takes two forms. The first and better-known type of misallocation arises because monopolies produce "too little," charging prices that exceed marginal costs, whereas the second type arises in the process of creating monopolies. Would-be monopolists spend resources in order to attain monopoly positions, and such expenditures are dissipating. The magnitude of these capture costs is comparable to that of the expected profits of the monopoly. Naturally, monopolists have economic rights to whatever gains they obtain. Since monopolists' gains exceed their contributions, their gains occur, in part, at the expense of others; thus, they also seem to have the right to harm other people. Yet such rights are not exercised indiscriminately, and it is worthwhile to determine the circumstances under which such power is likely to be used.

[1] A more detailed discussion of this problem may be found in Barzel 1994.

In general, a property that can be captured must lie, at least in part, in the public domain. Moreover, what lies in the public domain must have been relinquished by the previous owner. In the case at hand, if someone is able to capture a monopoly position or, more accurately, if someone is able to capture, at a resource cost, the rights to the monopoly gain, then the monopoly position itself must have been lying in the public domain. In order for these rights to have entered the public domain, individuals must have relinquished them in the first place. I am here attempting to delineate conditions under which individuals would allow this to happen where monopoly is attained by predatory pricing. In predatory pricing, an initially competitive industry is taken over by a predator, who monopolizes it by temporarily pricing the target commodity at less than it costs, thereby forcing the competitive producers to leave the industry or to sell their facilities cheaply to the predator. This method illustrates the general principle behind opportunities for capturing monopoly gains.[2]

In the competitive industry that exists before predatory action, consumers are able to purchase the target commodity from many sellers at a competitive price; this ability is threatened by the predator. Recalling that property rights are defined as an individual's ability to gain from the consumption and exchange of goods, it seems proper to ask what gives consumers the ability to obtain a good at the competitive price. Antimonopoly laws aside, consumers surely do not have a legal right to the competitive price. Consumers, however, can acquire the legal rights – and consequently the economic rights – by the simple expedient of signing long-term, competitively priced contracts for the commodity while the industry is competitive. They might choose to commit to such long-term contracts if they fear monopolization by a predator. Long-term contracts will also benefit the competitive sellers: It is difficult to ruin sellers who have signed such contracts, since they do not have to sell all their output at the predatory price; for the same reason, they command a high acquisition price from the predator.

As long as the extra costs of arranging long-term contracts over and above those of spot exchanges are less than the perceived loss to monopoly, threatened sellers and consumers will gain by establishing rights to supply and to be supplied, respectively, at the competitive price.[3] When the cost of protection, whether through long-term contracts or any other

---

[2] I here take no account of the controversy surrounding the logic of, and the evidence for, predatory practices.

[3] The successful predator will gain more (in present terms) from the ultimate monopoly pricing than she or he will lose from below-cost pricing during the predatory period or from buying out competitors at terms attractive to them. Conversely, consumers and preyed-upon firms will be the combined net losers from such predation, and it seems highly probable that consumers' losses from the monopoly price will exceed their gains from the initial lower price.

means, is less than the expected loss to being monopolized, the would-be monopolist cannot gain from the monopolization and therefore will not attempt it. In this sense the would-be predator does not possess the right to such a gain. Since the total losses the would-be monopolist inflicts on others exceeds his or her gain, as long as contracting costs are not high, the rights competitive buyers and sellers possess tend to be secure. Assuming that in the absence of defensive action the predatory practice is a real threat to competitive buyers and sellers, it is expected that the less costly it is to arrange long-term contracts in an industry, the less likely it is that the industry will be subject to monopolization.

In summary, the ability of consumers and competitive sellers to exchange at competitive prices depends on their own efforts to enforce the appropriate arrangements. By and large, they are expected to be successful because monopoly tends to be "dissipating" in the sense that the monopolist's gains are less than the costs he or she imposes on others. Still, when enforcement costs are high, consumers' and sellers' rights to be served at the competitive price are likely to be relinquished, and a predator may then capture the right to a monopoly position.

THE RELATIONSHIP BETWEEN PROPERTY RIGHTS AND THEFT

The existence of theft makes the distinction between economic and legal rights clear; it also highlights the notion that economic rights are never absolute. Thieves lack legal rights over the goods they steal. Nevertheless, they are able to consume the goods, to exclude others from using them, to derive income from them, and to alienate them. Each of these capabilities is an attribute of ownership. The lack of legal rights may reduce the value of these capabilities, but it does not nullify them.

The fact that thieves have rights over stolen property implies that the current owners of property that might possibly be stolen do not have full rights over "their" property. Owners cannot be certain of the future use of such properties. The economic rights they do have depend, in part, on the protection effort made by the state. These rights also depend on the measures owners take to protect themselves from theft: The more they are willing to spend, the more secure their rights are expected to become. The effort they make, however, is not expected to deter all theft. For instance, fences around orchards are not made to be totally insurmountable; the cost of making them insurmountable exceeds the gain. Here, too, individuals choose to leave some rights in the public domain. When the probability that thieves will steal one's apples is positive, then one has only partial ownership over the apples.

Private-protection methods are as varied as are commodities themselves. Owners of apple orchards may employ guards to reduce theft; they may place trees farther from their property boundaries than they would in the absence of theft; and they may grow less valuable apples that are less appealing to thieves. Indeed, landowners might grow entirely different crops if theft became a serious problem.[4] Those owners who wish to employ others to tend their orchards may fear employee theft. Changing a contract's form is expected to change the incentive to steal. If, for example, an owner forms a fixed-rent contract with a worker to tend the orchard, the problem of the worker's theft simply disappears.

The notion that theft is a manifestation of the imperfect delineation of rights can be illustrated by reconsidering movie theaters. Of the attributes theater owners relinquish to the public domain, two relate to the difference in value among seats. The first relinquished attribute is the difference in value between the better and the inferior seats within a price class of seats. People can capture the difference in value by arriving early and occupying the better seats. To the extent that policing is imperfect, a second attribute that is partially relinquished is the difference in value across price classes. Where seats are sold in several price classes, as is common outside the United States, buyers of lower-priced tickets can capture the difference to the extent that they are not prevented from occupying higher-priced seats. The state takes part in the enforcement effort only in the latter case, since jumping seats constitutes a legal infraction, whereas selecting a certain seat within a price class obviously does not. The economic logic of the two types of capture, however, is the same.

PROPERTY RIGHTS TO INNOVATIONS

In contrast to other areas in economics, the importance of property rights considerations to innovations has been widely recognized by economists; nevertheless, some major rights issues remain unresolved. One such issue concerns the economic rights innovators can expect to have over their innovations. When a uniquely talented individual develops an innovation, it seems plausible that such an individual will be able to obtain the rights to it, since he or she will control the field. On the other hand, if many individuals are able to develop the same innovation at a similar cost, it may appear that none has a right to it and that, in their competition for the gain from the innovation, its economic value will be dissipated; nevertheless, in this case rights may also be well defined.

A useful measure of the net present value of an innovation is the differ-

---

[4] Reportedly some avocado orchards in the San Diego area have been abandoned because of increased theft.

ence between total consumers' valuation and total innovators' costs. Each of the potential patterns of activity leading to a particular innovation will generate its own net present value. The highest value will be generated by the innovative activity that satisfies two conditions: that it be free of duplication and that it be undertaken at the time that yields the highest consumer valuation net of innovating costs. One market force that tends to bring about the realization of these conditions is competition among innovators in recruiting customers for their particular innovations before expending resources on the actual innovation.[5] In order to attract potential customers away from competing innovators, not only will innovators tend to cede to customers all the gains from the innovation, but the winning innovator will also be the one who performs the innovation activity closest to the time that maximizes its net present value; only then can the bid for customers dominate that of competitors. When the cost of recruiting customers, whether directly or indirectly, is low, customers have, in practice, the rights to the gain from the innovation. As in the case of predatory practices, the easier the advance contracting, the better the delineation of rights.

Innovators who possess unique talents do not need to cede to customers all the potential gains the innovations generate. Such innovators may encounter another problem, however. Every customer may try to obtain a bargain by offering the lowest royalty payment. Since the innovators' marginal cost of serving extra consumers is zero, they may be willing to relinquish ground rather than lose customers. Individuals' incentive for bargaining under these conditions implies that the difference between the maximum consumers' valuation and the marginal cost lies in the public domain. The potential loss from such bargaining can, however, be lowered if the parties can be compelled not to bargain. Therefore, if the option of selling the use of the innovation to different consumers at different prices can be eliminated, either privately or through legal prohibition of price discrimination, then the innovator's rights over the innovation will be partially restored. Maximizing sellers will equate their constrained marginal revenue to their (zero) marginal cost and will price accordingly. The superimposed uniformity of prices – royalty rates in this context – delineates rights, and their determination is free of direct capture costs. This arrangement is not entirely free of cost, however, because when a single price is prescribed, the welfare triangle that could have been avoided under price discrimination is relinquished to the public domain.

---

[5] Yu (1981) discusses at length methods used for such recruiting. Demsetz (1968) was the first to consider advance contracting for selling commodities whose production is subject to declining costs.

Economic analysis of property rights

PROPERTY RIGHTS TO PRICE INFORMATION

Coase (1937) notwithstanding, economists seldom realize that determining which prices will clear the market is a resource-consuming activity. Were such prices easy to determine, no serious errors in setting prices would occur, yet significant pricing errors are widespread. Some concerts, for example, are poorly attended, whereas tickets for others can be obtained only from scalpers. Likewise, some artists sell out at their gallery openings, but others see an entire show go by without selling a thing. Last, some new stock offerings are instantly snatched up, while others turn out to be duds. Such examples suggest that setting prices correctly is costly. Providing price estimates is costly as well and must generate a reward; since the estimates are subject to error, speculators may capture the value of the difference. Resources will be spent both on the capture of price information and on the prevention of such capture.

It might be expected that prices would be set by individuals who specialize in doing so, yet on examination the direct sale of price estimates proves problematic. If the producers were to purchase price estimates for their commodities, they would also require a guarantee of the quality of the service they were buying. Some of these commodity producers, however, could take advantage of the fact of the guarantee by lowering product quality and shifting part of the guarantee burden to the pricing specialist. This difficulty may be avoided if the producer of the commodity also sets the price, which might explain why the two activities are often performed within the same organization.

Some commodities and services are not as susceptible to the problem of guarantee abuse as others, and for these the producer of the price estimate may guarantee his or her service, thereby becoming the residual claimant to variability in the value of the service. An important example of the provision of price services by independent specialists may be seen in syndicates of investment bankers, which advise business firms about the price at which to sell new stock. At the heart of the transaction between a syndicate and an issuer of stock is the implicit price guarantee. Essentially, a syndicate buys the entire stock flotation at the agreed-upon price and offers it to the public at a price not exceeding a predetermined ceiling. A syndicate that errs by overestimating the market-clearing price will be the one to bear the effect of its error. The syndicate, then, maintains the property right to its price estimate.

Pricing errors may have an additional effect on behavior. The ultimate buyers of a new stock may either rely on the recommendation of the syndicate or devise their own (or use their advisers') estimates of the market price of a stock and act accordingly. The latter action constitutes a duplication of effort, since the information is a public good that has already been produced by the syndicate. The lower the costs associated with acquiring a stock, the greater the demand for it; the demand is also higher if buyers believe that, on average, their suppliers offer them bargains. They cannot, however, expect every new stock to be a bargain. Since some stocks are expected to be duds and others are expected to be bargains, buying only the latter and avoiding the former would be highly profitable. Information on new offerings that allows a speculator to avoid some of the duds while concentrating on the bargains should enable him or her to earn a positive return. Success by such a speculator, however, will lower the return to uninformed buyers; they will be forced to buy relatively more duds, since a relatively large fraction of the bargains will already have been purchased by the speculator. The demand for stocks by buyers who do not acquire information on individual issues but who are aware of the average return on new stocks will be lower when they must compete with speculators, resulting in lower stock prices.

In order to protect their rights from being captured by speculators and to prevent an adverse shift in the demand facing them, syndicates must deter speculators from acquiring information. This may explain the restrictions on the number of shares of a new issue individuals or organizations are allowed to purchase. If would-be speculators can use their information to buy only small blocks of shares, they will seldom find the information worth collecting. Thus, the restriction seems to protect the rights of syndicates to their costly price information.

PROPERTY RIGHTS TO WILDLIFE

Wildlife, by its very nature, is fleeting. How can one establish rights to it?[6] It would be simple to let one person own the entire habitat of a wildlife stock such as a herd of deer. Some large hunting ranches in the United States do contain the entire habitats of several wild animals, and some African game preserves are home to whole herds of many different species. Seemingly, the reason these ranches are so large is to encompass entire habitats. Likewise, many primitive societies seem to have owned the entire habitat of wildlife stock they hunted or fished.

A wildlife stock that occupies and traverses a land area is only one of several attributes of the land; the others include the capacity for growing wheat, yielding minerals and groundwater, and offering scenic vantage points, as well as providing habitat for wildlife. Each implies a distinct parcel size and shape for optimal use. Wildlife stocks themselves are diverse, varying greatly both in value (pests being negatively valued) and in the size of the territory they occupy. Were transaction costs zero – and

[6] The discussion in this section borrows heavily from Lueck 1989.

taking account of the interactions among the attributes – each would be optimally exploited and, consistent with the Coase Theorem, the owner-ship pattern would be irrelevant. Since transaction costs are positive, the ownership pattern matters. The ownership by single persons of entire habitats of migrating birds that travel across vast areas and of wildlife stocks that cover a wide swath precludes the ownership pattern that ac-commodates many small farms and other efficient-size land holdings. We would expect the ownership pattern that emerges to conform primarily to the most valued use of the land. This implies that in many instances the non-wildlife use of the land would take precedence. Government, however, can take action so as to enhance the value of such wildlife – and it would appear that it does.

The current legal doctrine governing wildlife in the United States as-signs the regulation of wildlife and its partial ownership to the states and sometimes to the federal government. Private individuals are also legal owners of some wildlife attributes, as well as being the economic owners of many of them. The allocation of rights to wildlife in Canada is similar to that in the United States. In England, however, these rights are mostly assigned to private individuals. The difference is consistent with the hy-pothesis that these governments attempt to maximize the value of wild-life.

Although the population density in England is considerably higher than it is in the United States and Canada, the average farm size is much larger in England than it is in the United States and Canada.[7] The habitat required to support the most valuable wildlife stocks in these three coun-tries displays the opposite pattern. Large mammals are rare in England, and game birds and fish tend to be local there; whereas in the United States and even more so in Canada the habitat of large mammals is vast, and many game birds and fishes migrate long distances. Whereas English law is the basis of law in the United States and Canada – law in the latter two, especially Canadian law, still has much in common with that in the former – the wildlife components of the American and Canadian laws diverge drastically from the English ones. In England, where holdings are large and wildlife habitats are modest, wildlife is not controlled by the state to a great degree, individuals holding the bulk of the rights to it. In the United States and Canada the law is much more restrictive regarding the rights to wildlife individuals have, and the states, provinces, and fed-eral authorities retain a much greater regulatory power than do their English counterparts. For example, the restrictions on the length of the

[7]For example, according to Lueck (1989) "in 1899, the mean farm size in the United Kingdom was 390 acres; it was 134 acres in the United States" (p. 312), and "private landholdings are even smaller and more scattered in Canada than in the United States" (pp. 316–17).

season, the bag limit, and the trade in wildlife products are much more severe in the United States and Canada than they are in England. It is worth noting that within the United States and Canada the rights retained by the states and provinces are relatively more local than those assumed by the federal authorities. Moreover, consistent with the notion that the purpose of the regulations is to maximize the value of wildlife, private ownership to wildlife in game farms and fish ponds is routinely granted. Whereas in the absence of government regulations, much of the roaming wildlife in the United States and Canada would be common property, the law reduces the overexploitation of such wildlife, thereby increasing its value to individuals. The need for such laws and regulations is much reduced in England, where individuals' land holdings conform quite closely to wildlife habitat.

11

The property rights model: Recapitulation

People have discretion over how to delineate rights, and as part of their maximization effort they do so to whatever degree they desire. Rights are never perfectly delineated, however, because the fact that commodities are not uniform and are expensive to measure makes perfect delineation prohibitively costly. Nevertheless, since people do what they deem "best," rights may be said to be always well delineated.

Those properties that people choose not to delineate are in the public domain. Such properties include much of the world's oceans; they also include the cool air in air-conditioned shopping malls, which is not charged for on the margin. Properties in the public domain can be augmented or diminished. As the values of commodities and of commodity attributes change, and as the costs of delineation and of protection change, people's decisions regarding what to leave in, what to relinquish, and what to reclaim from the public domain change correspondingly.

The public domain is ubiquitous; innumerable commodity attributes are placed in it. Any service not fully charged for on the margin is at least partly relinquished to the public domain. Owners could charge for such services, but the extra returns often do not justify the extra costs. For instance, concert-hall owners relinquish to the public domain the differential in valuation among equally priced seats. When the value of concert-hall seats falls – which might happen when the hall is used by a local choir rather than a famous opera star – seats are expected to be priced in lesser detail. The differences in value among seats that were formerly differentially priced are relinquished to the public domain. Patrons are expected to claim that differential through the expenditure of resources. Resource owners attempt to maximize the net values of their resources: They attempt to organize their actions so that, ceteris paribus, they minimize the losses from placing attributes in the public domain.

In order to gain from exchange, people must spend resources on transferring rights to commodities. Contracts are expected to be structured so as to minimize the costs of exchange of given transactions. In forming their contracts, transactors have a choice of units by which to regulate their transactions; for instance, labor can be exchanged by the hour or by the piece. The use of each of these units relinquishes different subsets of attributes to the public domain: the per-hour effort when labor is sold by the hour; the care or quality of the output when labor is sold by the piece.

In addition to having a choice of units, contractors may also impose restrictions on the way they conduct their exchanges in order to reduce the amount they spend to capture from each other. Refrigerator producers, for example, often make the sale of their merchandise subject to a warranty, while at the same time prohibiting buyers from using their refrigerators commercially. The warranty service is a free attribute to buyers in that they are not as heavily penalized for carelessness or for extra-heavy use as they would be if they had to pay for repairs themselves. The restriction serves to reduce such usage. The more valued transactions are, the more attributes are expected to be priced, or the more comprehensive the restrictions are expected to be.

Since exchanged commodities are not uniform and are not fully measured, the value of the exchange is variable. A contract allocates the variability in a transaction among the transactors. As transactors alter the units by which they effect exchange, and as they alter the associated restrictions, they also divide the variability in outcome among themselves differently. That allocation of variability which maximizes the contractor's wealth is the one wherein the ability of a contractor to affect the value of the mean outcome of the transaction is positively related to the share of variability he or she will assume. It is expected, for instance, that refrigerator manufacturers will assume variability in income by guaranteeing more comprehensively those aspects of their refrigerators' performance that are most affected by their production procedures yet least likely to be affected by consumers' actions. As was noted earlier, whereas a refrigerator's paint is guaranteed for only a short period, the warranty on its motor remains in force for several years.

All sales, with the exception of some governed by caveat emptor, require organization. In sales subject to caveat emptor, buyers need assurances that they will not walk away with worthless merchandise. If buyers check directly, the degree of organization may be trivial. Not trivial, however, is the resource cost of such exchanges. Non–caveat emptor sales, that is, sales in which the transactors have imposed constraints on each other, require real organization in order to police and to monitor the constraints. The nature of, and the costs associated with, such organizations vary with the pricing method used. A change in conditions, such as a change in the valuation of the transacted commodity, is expected to change the method by which the commodity is sold, as well as the organizational structure governing its exchange.

Who will post the price at which to commit to trade, the seller or the buyer? This theory yields the implication that whichever party can better predict prices will be the one to post them. Whoever posts a price subjects himself or herself to exploitation; his or her exchange partners may engage in excessive price prediction, discover prediction errors, and take advantage of the willingness to deal at a fixed price. It is further implied that the person who can more readily predict the price will be the one who will have to assume the consequences of posting it. Price prediction is subject to economies of scale; the more units traded at that price, the lower the unit cost of the prediction. Thus, as the size of the buyer vis-à-vis the seller increases, the more likely are buyers, whose unit cost of prediction has declined, to post prices at which they agree to purchase what sellers wish to sell.

Because all but the lowest-value transactions are subject to constraint and require organization, only a small fraction of transactions are "in the market," as this term is usually understood. The frequently asked question as to which transactions will take place in the market and which will remain within the firm is not likely to receive a useful answer, however. Firm transactions are not uniform, and some of them are more in the firm than others. A more fruitful question concerns the determination of the forms of organizations that will govern different kinds of transactions and of the forces that will bring about change to these organizations.

The complexity of commodities and activities causes ownership patterns to be complex as well. The most efficient owner of a particular commodity attribute is not necessarily the most efficient owner of the commodity's other attributes. It may be advantageous to split the ownership of a commodity among several individuals. Because the commodity is itself not physically split, each owner, if not properly constrained, may find it easy to consume some of the others' unpriced attributes. In the previously mentioned restriction on the commercial use of refrigerators, the owner of the attribute "warranty service" restricts the behavior of the owners of some of the refrigerator's other attributes.

Organizations, including business firms, typically engage in a multitude of activities, including policing and monitoring constraints. In the case of the business firm, many factors affect the variability in its income. The price of each commodity it buys or sells can fluctuate, each specimen of the commodities it exchanges may differ from others, and its income may depend on whether or not such phenomena as fires, earthquakes, and foreign confiscations occur. Each of these instances of income variability may be borne by a different party. A firm may purchase a raw material on the spot market, or it may operate under a long-term, fixed-price contract for it. Assuming no breach of contract, in the former case the buying firm bears the effect of fluctuations in the price of the commodity; in the latter case its contract insures it against fluctuations. These considerations apply to all the firm's sources of variability. In each of these instances it is expected that the party that is better able to affect the mean outcome will tend to assume the associated variability. For example, it is expected that a raw-material supplier that has some power to set its price is more likely to sign fixed-price, long-term contracts than one not possessing such power.

Similar considerations apply to labor services. Workers, who can affect outcome-value more easily than the purchaser of the labor services can, are likely to operate as independent contractors selling output rather than labor. At the other extreme, purchasers of labor services will assume variability in outcome by paying a fixed wage on a long-term basis. It is to be expected that as the market wage of workers rises, they will gravitate toward self-employment.[1]

When two parties agree to a formula for dividing future income variability, one may emerge as the winner and the other as the loser as the outcome of the transaction unfolds. Because the loser could gain by reneging on the contract, each party demands assurances from the other that the contract will not be breached. A necessary though insufficient condition for such assurances is that a party be able to meet his or her obligations. Fixed-wage suppliers of labor can readily guarantee performance even when the market wage exceeds the contract wage, because they own their own labor services. The employer of such workers must be able to ensure wage payment when the market wage falls below the contract wage. Equity capital specializes in providing such assurances. More generally, it seems that equity capital is assembled (and augmented) in order to guarantee all the contracts signed by the firm. These contracts may, in turn, be viewed as constituting the firm; in this sense shareholders are the owners of the firm, and the firm is a "nexus of contracts."

CONCLUSION

I have attempted to demonstrate how the property rights transaction cost model can generate a better understanding of the allocation of resources and of the interaction of this allocation with economic organization. The literature that assumes that the costs of transacting are zero and that all

[1] Barzel 1987.

property rights are perfectly well delineated is incapable of dealing with a vast array of actual observed practices. Particularly glaring is the inability of such an approach to explain why exchange parties would ever impose restrictions on each other. The property rights approach is capable of addressing such issues.

Many approaches to the analysis of economic behavior do not explicitly assume that transaction costs are zero, but they also do not inquire as to what the precise rights of the parties are. It is my impression that economists who neglect property rights considerations are prone to making implicit assumptions that are often not well taken, while producing results that are hard to accept. It is quite common to find cases where within single models some transaction costs are implicitly assumed to be zero (e.g., it is routinely assumed that monopolists know precisely what their demand is) while others are assumed to be prohibitively expensive (e.g., it is routinely assumed that price discrimination by monopolists is prohibitively costly).[2] The approach that insists on asking who owns every particular attribute of a commodity and what "owners" can actually do with "their" commodities seems to come closer to the root of transaction costs and is, therefore, less likely to fall prey to untenable assumptions.

Finally, consider the application of the property rights approach to the distribution of gains from trade. Many goods are valued less by their current owners than they are by other individuals. Who owns these potential gains from trade? In the competitive, zero transaction cost model, the distribution of the gains is costlessly determined. The costless information (or the uniformity of commodities) necessary for such competition is, however, seldom encountered in reality. Opportunities for people to gain at the expense of others seem ubiquitous. Whereas individuals are always ready to expend resources to increase their share of the pie, they will also seek out methods and organizations by which to better delineate rights to it, thereby dividing the pie without shrinking it too much.

A considerable portion of this book has been devoted to analyzing such behavior. It is fitting to conclude by visiting one unlikely place where the time and effort of haggling over the distribution of the gains from trade are effectively avoided: an Egyptian bazaar. To quote Werner (1987), in Cairo's "principal livestock market, camels take center stage. . . . [T]he camel market's own King Solomon [is] Muhammad Abd al-Aziz. . . . Sales are conducted one-on-one – one buyer, one seller and one

---

[2] Another example occurs in asymmetry-of-information models, where one set of individuals is, as a rule, implicitly assumed to be costlessly informed, while for others the information cost is assumed to be prohibitive.

camel at a time. . . . With an acutely discriminating sense of camel flesh [Muhammad] sets a fair price. . . . His authority is usually sufficient to settle any difference." Transaction costs are near zero in this particular market. Nothing, however, comes free. Here the cost in question is "a small margin for [Muhammad's] commission" (p. 132).

References

Akerlof, George. 1970, "The Market for 'Lemons': Quality Uncertainty and the Market Mechanism." *Quarterly Journal of Economics* 84: 488–500.

Alchian, Armen A. 1965. "Some Economics of Property Rights." *Il Politico* 30, no. 4: 816–29. Reprinted in Armen A. Alchian, *Economic Forces at Work.* Indianapolis, Ind.: Liberty Press, 1977.

Alchian, Armen A. 1987. "Property Rights." In *The New Palgrave: A Dictionary of Economics.* New York: Norton.

Alchian, Armen A., and William R. Allen. 1977. *Exchange and Production,* 2nd ed. Belmont, Calif.: Wadsworth.

Alchian, Armen A., and Harold Demsetz. 1972. "Production, Information Costs, and Economic Organization." *American Economic Review* 62, no. 5: 777–95.

Allen, Douglas W. 1991a. "Homesteading and Property Rights; or 'How the West Was Really Won.' " *Journal of Law and Economics* 24, no. 1: 1–23.

Allen, Douglas W. 1991b. "What Are Transaction Costs?" *Research in Law and Economics* 14: 1–18.

Allen, Douglas W., and Dean Lueck. 1992. "Contract Choice in Modern Agriculture: Cropshare Versus Cash Rent." *Journal of Law and Economics* 35, no. 2: 397–426.

Allen, Douglas W., and Dean Lueck, 1993. "Transaction Costs and the Design of Cropshare Contracts." *Rand Journal of Economics* 24, no. 1: 78–100.

Allen, George C. 1966 [1929]. *The Industrial Development of Birmingham and the Black Country, 1860–1927.* New York: Kelley.

Anderson, Terry L., and P. J. Hill, 1975. "The Evolution of Property Rights: A Study of the American West." *Journal of Law and Economics* 18, no. 1: 163–79.

Arrow, Kenneth J. 1973. "Higher Education as Filter." *Journal of Public Economics* 2, no. 3: 193–216.

Barzel, Yoram. 1974. "A Theory of Rationing by Waiting," *Journal of Law and Economics* 17, no. 1: 73–96.

Barzel, Yoram. 1977. "An Economic Analysis of Slavery." *Journal of Law and Economics* 20, no. 1: 87–110.

Barzel, Yoram. 1982. "Measurement Cost and the Organization of Markets." *Journal of Law and Economics* 25, no. 1: 27–48.

Barzel, Yoram. 1985. "Transaction Costs: Are They Just Costs?" *Journal of Institutional and Theoretical Economics* 141, no. 1: 4–16.

Barzel, Yoram. 1987. "The Entrepreneur's Reward for Self-Policing." *Economic Inquiry* 25, no. 1: 103–16.

References

Barzel, Yoram. 1994. "The Capture of Wealth by Monopolists and the Protection of Property Rights." *International Review of Law and Economics* 14: 292–409.

Barzel, Yoram, and Tim Sass. 1990. "The Allocation of Resources by Voting." *Quarterly Journal of Economics* 105: 745–71.

Bean, Richard N., and Robert P. Thomas. 1974. "The Profits of the Slave Trade: The Fishers of Men." *Journal of Economic History* 34, no. 4: 885–914.

Cheung, Steven N. S. 1969. *A Theory of Share Tenancy.* Chicago: University of Chicago Press.

Cheung, Steven N. S. 1974. "A Theory of Price Control." *Journal of Law and Economics* 17, no. 1: 53–72.

Cheung, Steven N. S. 1977. "Why Are Better Seats 'Underpriced'?" *Economic Inquiry* 15, no. 3: 513–22.

Cheung, Steven N. S. 1983. "The Contractual Nature of the Firm." *Journal of Law and Economics* 2, no. 1: 1–22.

Coase, Ronald H. 1937. "The Nature of the Firm." *Economica* 4, no. 3: 386–405.

Coase, Ronald H. 1960. "The Problem of Social Cost." *Journal of Law and Economics* 3, no. 1: 1–44.

Dahlman, Carl J. 1980. *The Open Field System and Beyond: A Property Rights Analysis of an Economic Institution.* Cambridge: Cambridge University Press.

Dam, Kenneth W. 1965. "Oil and Gas Licensing and the North Sea." *Journal of Law and Economics* 8, no. 2: 51–76.

Deacon, Robert T., and Jon Sonstelie. 1985. "Rationing by Waiting and the Value of Time: Results from a Natural Experiment." *Journal of Political Economy* 93, no. 4: 627–47.

Demsetz, Harold. 1967. "Toward a Theory of Property Rights." *American Economic Review* 57, no. 2: 347–59.

Demsetz, Harold. 1968. "Why Regulate Utilities?" *Journal of Law and Economics* 11, no. 1: 55–66.

Eggertsson, Thráinn. 1990. *Economic Behavior and Institutions.* Cambridge: Cambridge University Press.

Ellickson, Robert C. 1991. *Order Without Law.* Cambridge, Mass.: Harvard University Press.

Eswaran, Mukesh, and Ashok Kotwal. 1985. "A Theory of Contractual Structure in Agriculture." *American Economic Review* 75, no. 3: 352–67.

Fogel, Robert William, and Stanley L. Engerman. 1972. *Time on the Cross: The Economics of American Negro Slavery.* Boston: Little, Brown.

Gisser, Micha. 1995. "The Evolvement of Water Rights: Testing the Barzel Rule." Mimeographed.

Goldberg, Victor P. 1985. "Production Functions, Transaction Costs, and the New Institutionality." In *Issues in Contemporary Economics,* ed. E. Feiwel, 395–402. New York: Macmillan.

Gordon, H. Scott. 1954. "The Economics of a Common Property Resource: The Fishery." *Journal of Political Economy* 62, no. 2: 124–42.

Grossman, Sanford, and Oliver Hart. 1986. "The Cost and Benefits of Ownership: A Theory of Vertical and Lateral Integration." *Journal of Political Economy* 94, no. 4: 691–719.

Hall, Christopher D. 1986. "Market Enforced Information Asymmetry: A Study of Claiming Races." *Economic Inquiry* 24, no. 2: 271–91.

References

Hart, Oliver, and John Moore. 1990. "Property Rights and the Nature of the Firm." *Journal of Political Economy* 48, no. 6: 1119–58.

Holmstrom, Bengt R., and Paul Milgrom. 1991. "Multitask Principal-Agent Analysis: Incentive Contracts, Asset Ownership and Job Design." *Journal of Law, Economics and Organization* 7: 24–52.

Holmstrom, Bengt R., and Paul Milgrom. 1994. "The Firm as an Incentive System." *American Economic Review* 84, no. 4: 972–91.

Jensen, Michael C., and William H. Meckling. 1976. "Theory of the Firm: Managerial Behavior, Agency Costs and Ownership Structure." *Journal of Financial Economics* 3, no. 3: 305–60.

Johnson, Ronald N., Micha Gisser, and Michael Werner. 1981. "The Definition of a Surface Water Right and Transferability." *Journal of Law and Economics* 24, no. 2: 273–88.

Kalt, Joseph P. 1981. *The Economics and Politics of Oil Price Regulation: Federal Policy in the Post-Embargo Era.* Cambridge, Mass.: MIT Press.

Kessel, Reuben A. 1974. "Transfused Blood, Serum Hepatitis, and the Coase Theorem." *Journal of Law and Economics* 17, no. 2: 265–90.

Klein, Benjamin, Robert G. Crawford, and Armen A. Alchian. 1978. "Appropriable Rents, Vertical Integration, and the Competitive Contracting Process." *Journal of Law and Economics* 21, no. 2: 297–326.

Knight, Frank H., 1921. *Risk, Uncertainty and Profit.* Boston: Houghton Mifflin.

Knight, Frank H. 1924. "Some Fallacies in the Interpretation of Social Cost." *Quarterly Journal of Economics* 38, no. 7: 582–606.

Krueger, Anne O. 1974. "The Political Economy of the Rent-Seeking Society." *American Economic Review* 66, no. 3: 291–303.

Landes, William M. 1971. "An Economic Analysis of the Courts." *Journal of Law and Economics* 14, no. 1: 61–108.

Libecap, Gary D. 1989. *Contracting for Property Rights.* Cambridge: Cambridge University Press.

Lueck, Dean. 1989. "The Economic Nature of Wildlife Law." *Journal of Legal Studies* 18, no. 2: 291–324.

Milgrom, Paul, and John Roberts. 1990. "The Economics of Modern Manufacturing: Technology Strategy and Organization." *American Economic Review* 80, no. 3: 511–28.

Miller, Kathleen A. 1985. "The Right to Use vs. the Right to Sell: Water Rights in the Western United States." Ph.D. diss., University of Washington.

North, Douglass C. 1981. *Structure and Change in Economic History.* New York: Norton.

Ostrom, Elinor. 1990. *Governing the Common: The Evolution of Institutions for Collective Action.* Cambridge: Cambridge University Press.

Posner, Richard A. 1975. "The Social Cost of Monopoly and Regulation." *Journal of Political Economy* 83, no. 4: 807–27.

Posner, Richard A. 1992. *Economic Analysis of Law.* 4th ed., Boston: Little, Brown.

Priest, George L. 1980. "Selective Characteristics of Litigation." *Journal of Legal Studies* 9, no. 1: 399–421.

Priest, George L., and Benjamin Klein. 1984. "The Selection of Disputes for Litigation." *Journal of Legal Studies* 13, no. 1: 1–56.

Rockoff, Hugh. 1984. *Drastic Measures: A History of Wage and Price Controls in the United States.* Cambridge: Cambridge University Press.

References

Rose, Carol M. 1990. "Energy and Efficiency in the Realignment of Common-Law Water Rights." *Journal of Legal Studies* 19, no. 2: 261–96.

Ross, Stephen A. 1973. "The Economic Theory of Agency: The Principal's Problem." *American Economic Review* 63, no. 2: 134–39.

Silberberg, Eugene. 1990. *The Structure of Economics*. 2nd ed., New York: McGraw Hill.

Spence, A. Michael. 1973. "Job Market Signaling." *Quarterly Journal of Economics* 87, no. 4: 355–79.

Stigler, George J. 1966. *The Theory of Price*. 3rd ed., New York: Macmillan.

Tullock, Gordon. 1967. "The Welfare Cost of Tariffs, Monopolies and Theft." *Western Economic Journal* 5, no. 3: 224–32.

Umbeck, John. 1977. "The California Gold Rush: A Study of Emerging Property Rights." *Explorations in Economic History* 14, no. 2: 197–206.

Umbeck, John. 1981. "Might Makes Right: A Theory of the Formation and Initial Distribution of Property Rights." *Economic Inquiry* 19, no. 1: 38–59.

Varian, Hal R. 1992. *Microeconomic Analysis*. 3rd ed., New York: Norton.

Werner, Louis. 1987. "North to Cairo along the Schorching Way of the Forty." *Smithsonian* (March): 120–33.

Williamson, Oliver E. 1975. *Markets and Hierarchies: Analysis and Antitrust Implications*. New York: Free Press.

Williamson, Oliver E. 1985. *The Economic Institutions of Capitalism*. New York: Free Press.

Yu, Ben T. 1981. "Potential Competition and Contracting in Innovation." *Journal of Law and Economics* 24, no. 2: 215–39.

Index

ad valorem tax, 34
agency theory, 14
Akerlof, George, 15n
Alchian, Armen A., 3, 4n, 6n, 14,
    65n, 75–6, 93n, 124n
Allen, Douglas W., 3n, 4n, 33n, 43n,
    46n, 122n, 123n
Allen, George C., 56n
Allen, William R., 3, 4n, 93n
allocation by government, 132–8
Anderson, Terry L., 119n
Arrow, Kenneth J., 14n
asset specificity, 14

Barzel, Yoram, 4n, 6n, 17n, 43n, 76,
    103n, 106n, 130n, 139n, 151n
Bean, Richard N., 105n
blood, donated, 130–2

California gold rush, 85–6
caveat emptor transactions, 72–3, 80
charity, 130–2
Cheung, Steven N. S., 3, 14, 19n, 21,
    30, 33–6, 44, 65n, 73–6, 81, 94n,
    122n
Coase, Ronald H., 7, 14, 65, 72–7,
    84, 144
Coase Theorem, 7, 9, 36, 77, 98, 102,
    108, 146
command economy, 136n
common law, 98–9
common property, 56, 62–4, 89–90,
    99–101, see also public domain
Crawford, Robert G., 14n, 65n, 75–6,
    124n

Dahlman, Carl J., 99, 100n
Dam, Kenneth W., 101
Deacon, Robert T., 25n
Demsetz, Harold, 15, 65n, 75, 91–2,
    143n
dispute resolution, 96–9
dissipation, minimization of, 29–32
divided ownership, 6–7, 55–64, 115–
    17
donated blood, 130–2

economic rights defined, 3, 90
Eggertsson, Thráinn, 13n
Ellickson, Robert C., 3, 90n
emergence of rights, 86–9
emergence of state, 86–9
Engerman, Stanley L., 110
equity capital, 80–4
Eswaran, Mukesh, 40n, 51n

firm, theories of, 75–7
fixed-rent contract, 40–9
Fogel, Robert W., 110
Fogelquist, Del, 20n

George, Henry, 39n
Gisser, Micha, 121n
gold rush, 85–6
Goldberg, Victor P., 67n
Gordon, H. Scott, 14, 89
Grossman, Sanford, 75–6
guarantee capital, 80–4

Hall, Christopher D., 61n
Hart, Oliver, 75–6

159

Index

Hill, P. J., 119n
Hobbes, Thomas, 86–8
Holmstrom, Bengt R., 40n, 75–6
homesteading, 121–3

indentured servitude, 105–6, 113
innovations, 142–3
insurance, 60–2

Jensen, Michael C., 4n, 14n, 65n
Jewish law, 112n
Johnson, Ronald N., 121n

Kalt, Joseph P., 20n
Kessel, Reuben A., 130–2
Klein, Benjamin, 14n, 65n, 75–6, 99n, 124n
Knight, Frank H., 14, 65, 68, 89, 100
Kotwal, Ashok, 40n, 51n
Krueger, Anne O., 14n

labor input, 66–72
   slaves', 106–8
Landes, William M., 99n
legal rights defined, 4, 90
liability, 77
Libecap, Gary D., 92n
Lueck, Dean, 33n, 46n, 101n, 118n, 145n, 146n

market signaling, 14
market transactions defined, 73
Meckling, William H., 4n, 14n, 65n
Milgrom, Paul, 40n, 75–6
Miller, Kathleen A., 118n
monopoly, 139–41
Moore, John, 75–6

National Football League, 5
non-market allocation, 128–38
North, Douglass C., 89n
North Sea, rights to, 101–2

Ostrom, Elinor, 99n
ownership
   allocation of, 7–9, 48
   divided, 6–7, 55–64, 115–17

Peterson, Bruce, 20n, 26n
police protection, 117–18
Posner, Richard A., 6n, 14n

predatory pricing, 139–41
price control, 18–32, 136
price information, 144–5
Priest, George L., 99n
property rights
   to prices, 144–5
   to wildlife, 145–7
   see also economic rights defined; legal rights defined
public domain, 5, 16–32, 97

quasi rents, 14

rationing by waiting, 16–18
rent seeking, 14
rents, quasi, 14
Roberts, John, 75–6
Rockoff, Hugh, 20n
Rose, Carol M., 118n
Ross, Stephen A., 14n

Sass, Tim, 130n
share contract, 33–7, 49–51, 58–9
signaling, market, 14
Silberberg, Eugene, 44n
slavery, 1, 105–13
slaves' consumption, 110–11
slaves' supervision cost, 108–10
Sonstelie, Jon, 25n
specializing, gains from, 51–2
Spence, A. Michael, 14n
Suen, Wing, 129n
supervision costs of slaves, 108–10
supply, firm and industry, 69–70

tax, ad valorem, 34
tax distortion, 34, 49
theft, 90, 111–13, 117–18, 141–2
Thomas, Robert P., 105n
transaction costs, 5
   defined, 4
Tullock, Gordon, 14n

Umbeck, John, 14, 85, 90, 94–5

Varian, Hal R., 66n
vertical integration, 123–6
voting, 100, 129–30

wage contract, 48, 63–4
   variability in, 78–80

Index